LANDESMAN'S LEGACY

LANDESMAN'S LEGACY

The Abandoned Writings

Arranged by

Richard Schain

ΓΠ
Garric Press
Glen Ellen, CA

Copyright © 2018 Richard Schain

All rights reserved. No part of this book may be reproduced without written permission from the author, except for the use of brief quotations in a book review.

Printed in the United States of America

First Printing, 2018

ISBN 978-0-9609922-4-9

Extracts from the Legacy

"I imagine my soul to become a building block of some divine spiritual structure, perhaps even a keystone for some spiritual archway. I have been called upon to develop this soul of mine to its maximum potential. It is a *spiritual instinct* analogous to the instincts that drive migratory birds to fly over continents. I don't have to know why I have this instinct; I only am compelled to follow it to the best of my ability."

"Either one takes seriously one's own metaphysical soul or one restricts oneself to superficial material being. Either a human being is a soul dragging around its little corpse or a material body with an illusory epiphenomenon called a soul (the view of contemporary psychology). There can be no intermediate position."

"The necessity for spiritual awareness is greater than ever before. Yet it is continuously shrinking in an age of materialism and mechanization. One can imagine that the only hope for an individual is *transfiguration* of his soul at the end of his life and its entry into a metaphysical dimension of existence."

"For me, the highest attainment of culture is a deepening consciousness of one's self, of one's soul, and its relationship to a metaphysical ground of existence (in a word, God), a goal that is generally ignored today. One may properly call this concept 'mysticism', even though the word is held in ill repute in contemporary intellectual circles. However, regardless of ill repute, the task of a relevant philosophy is the transmutation of mystical consciousness into coherent concepts that can enlighten the soul and be able to be transmitted to others."

"These writings I produce are not like any other of which I am aware. They are not a diary of events in my life, they are not literary memoirs, they are not a journal like that of Thoreau, recording his daily observations of nature, and they are certainly not confessions. I have nothing to confess. What they are, I believe, are *catalysts* for my metaphysical development. They may not have started that way, but that is what they have become. If this development should end, I would write no more."

"A hypothetical questioner criticizes me—who am I, a failed academician, a recluse living in a forest, a writer without readers—who am I to make such sweeping condemnations of my society! My answer is—I am who I am, I feel what I must, I think what my feelings tell me to think, and I freely write what I think. A place has been assigned to me in this world as I am; others can find their own place in it."

"Finding a valuable book is like finding a pearl in oysters, one has to crack open a great many to find one that is truly enlivening. No doubt that is why Marcus Aurelius says "Away with books!" early in his meditations. But if one had listened to Marcus, he never would have read his Meditations…Books that enliven, enlighten, and enrich one's soul exist; they should be sought after and treasured like valuable pearls."

"The painful truth, as I see it, is that individuals do not value their own unique selves as much as they should, and they give themselves over to any cause that relieves them of the burden of self-valuation. What is necessary is not superficial selfishness, but self-respect in its deepest meaning, respect for one's own soul."

Dedicated to

those individuals

who tend to their soul

INTRODUCTION

Leon Landesman, sometime before his demise, had sent me a manuscript by post, which was published by Paragon House in 2016 under the title *Landesman's Journal*. Landesman's history and the circumstances of his solitary life are described in the introduction to the *Journal*. Briefly, he had been a college instructor in philosophy somewhere in the East, but he had found the life unrewarding and had moved to southern Arizona where he took a job in a rural post office. Years later (the dating is unclear), he left his position, purchased an isolated cabin on the edge of the Coronado National Forest near the Mexican border, and embarked on a life of solitude. *Landesman's Journal* was the record he had sent to me of his intense interior life setting forth his thoughts about himself and about the world in which he had lived.

The present writings have a very different history. Landesman had been a neighbor with whom I was acquainted, albeit a neighbor living some miles away. After his death, I took to using his abandoned cabin as a resting place during my daily walk with my dogs. In some way, I felt this to be my homage to him. One day, I noticed a structure well behind his cabin that I had not been aware of previously. It was an old shed, in a state of marked disrepair, fronted by a broken door. On an impulse, I pushed open the door and walked in. It was dark inside but I could see rusted tools scattered about. I was about to leave when I noticed an old trunk with a painted dome exterior, revealing it to be a relic of former times. With some effort, I opened it. It was filled with old clothing; however, on one side was a tattered, bulging red portfolio held together with string. Since I knew the property had been completely abandoned, I didn't hesitate to take it home with me.

The portfolio was filled with Landesman's writings, printed out on odd sheets of paper. I could tell the printing had been done with his ancient word processor, since the style looked exactly the same as the manuscript he had mailed to me. However, unlike the manuscript of *Landesman's Journal*, everything was in disarray. Landesman had obviously not taken the care with these papers as he had with his journal.

I straightened out handfuls of the papers and began to read. It seemed to me that they were more forceful, more assertive than those from the *Journal*. After a short time, it became clear that these writings were at least at the same level of philosophical interest as the ones I had formerly received—perhaps even more so. Landesman must have arbitrarily taken some of his recent writings he was willing to reveal and sent them to me in journal format; however, the pages in front of me now were different in nature from the *Journal*. They demonstrate an uninhibited mystical side of himself that he may not have wanted to expose to the general public. They may not exhibit high literary virtuosity. However, I believe they are evidence of his remarkable insights into his own nature and the nature of the society in which he lived and, in the absence of any explicit prohibition on his part, they warrant being made available to interested readers.

As before, the pages were all undated, although some clearly followed others in the trend of their thought. I had the suspicion from their content that a few were written *after* he had mailed off his original manuscript to me. I have arranged and numbered them as best I could. Occasional editorial comments of mine are enclosed in brackets. Although Landesman quotes from my own writings, there are some unflattering descriptions of me in these pages that distressed me to read. I must confess that I was tempted to delete or at least to alter them, but I did not want to follow the example of Nietzsche's sister who removed unpleasant comments about herself from the manuscript of Nietzsche's last book *Ecce Homo*. Landesman's opinions about me have been left in their original form. I have entitled the writings *Landesman's Legacy* because after spending much time reading them, I regard them as a legacy to me personally and to anyone else who involves himself with the personality of Leon Landesman.

I have little to add to what I have said in *Landesman's Journal* about Landesman's innovative thinking and style of expression. In my view (in spite of his comments about me), he breaks new ground in philosophy, with original existential as well as historical perspectives. Recognition of him may not happen in the near future, as the entire current of philosophical thinking in this country flows in a far distant channel. Landesman was the epitome of a person living and writing *à rebours*. It is just as well that he does not achieve any widespread notoriety, because he would writhe in misery if he thought his writings were ever to fall into the hands of pedantic critics. There are clearly many repetitions in these writings. Landesman would say this should be regarded as a virtue, since new thoughts must be repeated to oneself many times to be assimilated into one's soul.

These are the last writings of Landesman that will appear in print. As Pushkin sadly said of Eugene Onegin, so I say to my alter ego, Leon Landesman, "Leon, I take my leave of you."

I am indebted to my wife Melanie Dreisbach who, with her usual editorial expertise, helped arrange and improved the final manuscript.

Richard Schain
Sonoita AZ, 2018

THE WRITINGS

~ 1 ~

I have been at odds with my society in one way or another for as long as I can remember. During the 1930s, at a vulnerable stage in my childhood when I was hardly aware of my Jewish origins, my parents arranged for our family to live for an unknown reason in an overtly anti-Semitic neighborhood. Hitler's doctrine that the Jew was the enemy of *society* was prevalent at that time in many circles in America. The scars from this period in my life are with me still. The feeling of alienation from my surroundings has been my greatest burden but also has been an inestimable benefit to me. It has allowed my soul to develop to its fullest extent; yet it has also involved pain and paranoia for me.

Although I have been writing philosophy for most of my adult life, I have not experienced 'success' as the term is commonly understood. Since there is no interest in my writings, 'no fish in the lake' as Nietzsche viewed the absence of readers, I have told myself to stop peering down into dead waters and instead cast my eyes upward to the firmament where there might be something metaphysical to be seen by a discerning viewer. If I can find no metaphysical dimension in which my soul exists, I might as well call it quits as a philosopher and descend into the banality of daily life—and soon the grave.

Either one takes seriously one's own metaphysical soul or one restricts oneself to superficial material being. Either a human being is a soul dragging around its little corpse or a material body with an illusory epiphenomenon called a soul (the view of contemporary psychology). There can be no intermediate position.

~ 2 ~

The degree to which commercialism dominates American art and literature today is unbearable. What can become of a nation if an almighty dollar tyrannizes over all aspects of it? The USA will end up like the Ottoman Empire, a termite-destroyed structure. It is not creation of wealth that is needed today; it is creation of art and literature that is meaningful to the human condition. But what is meaningful? That is the perennial question that occupies me. My faith is that if I keep writing, perhaps it may become clear to me.

Here I am, a *philosophe maudit*, contemplating a season in hell to improve my metaphysical prospects. But my bourgeois mentality and habits have held me back. *Gottenyue, hilf mir!* Eternity, I have need of you!

~ 3 ~

Eschatological Digression (last things). Scientists say that our sun will burn itself up some millions of years from now, which event will definitively end the history of our world. But one does not have to resort to astrophysics to realize life will radically change on the planet. Well before the solar holocaust, overpopulation, nuclear catastrophes, depletion of foodstuffs, climatic changes, and not least of all, the ever-widening gap between the rich and poor will bring to an end human civilization as we in developed societies know it. The various economic, social, and political remedies proposed by clever men will not avail. Robotization of our activities can only worsen the crisis. An individual must look squarely to his own life and not assume subsequent generations will give meaning to it, either in terms of progeny or of memories.

The necessity for spiritual awareness is greater than ever before. Yet it is continuously shrinking in an age of materialism and mechanization. One can imagine that the only hope for an individual is *transfiguration* of his soul at the end of his life and its entry into a metaphysical dimension of existence. This may seem far-fetched but it is no more far-fetched than the emergence of a soul in an individual human being. It is to be anticipated that transfiguration will not be automatic but will require prior preparation. Perhaps the purpose of physical life is this preparation. Not all will succeed in it. Every farmer who sows knows that only a few seeds will grow into plants. Only a few acorns become oak trees. Spiritually aware individuals intuit the compelling necessity for cultivation of their souls during their lifetime.

One can go even further and imagine that transfiguration consists of souls being incorporated into an ultimate spiritual reality named Divinity or God. They will act to *enrich* Him-Her. Souls can be compared to tributaries flowing into a great river. But not all reach the great river—many peter out en route. Thus one can envision that God needs human beings as much as they need Him—as was written by Abraham Joshua Heschel in his remarkable books.

I believe the essential goal of Homo sapiens is to form an independent soul, strong in creativity and durability. If this does not occur in a human life, it can be deemed a failure – like a fruit tree that yields shriveled fruit. An independent soul contributes to Divinity; a soul that is slave to biology and society is useless to it. If the human race stops producing independent, creative souls, it will no longer be viable and will die out. One can conceive of God as a great spiritual power in need of external fulfillment. Developed human souls are centers of spirituality and contribute to divine fulfillment. Some contribute much, others little or nothing. This idea, ridiculous to my peers, is acceptable to my intellectual conscience.

Individual physical immortality is a childish concept and should be discarded along with the myths associated with it. They derive from earlier stages of human mental development. Transmigration of souls (metempsychosis) seems an improbable idea but not an impossible consequence for souls that have not yet developed themselves. One must respect a metaphysical belief that has persisted for millennia in Eastern religions.

Whatever one thinks of last things, I believe development of one's soul is the most important task facing human beings. It is not religious conversion, not improving socioeconomic systems, not loving, helping, or instructing others. It is in forming one's own soul. Those who do not take their own souls *seriously,* do not *revere* it, cannot succeed in this task.

~ 4 ~

I have been feeling it necessary to get a handle on my life. There are too many things filling my mind and dragging it down. Repairing my roof, buying provisions for the kitchen, propane for the stove, dog food for Amigo, and others too trivial to even mention. What is it that I am about? That I should be about? When I take the time to unburden myself of these thoughts and contemplate my existence, it becomes clear to me what I am after, what I always have been after—*the formation of my soul*. At my age, one might think my soul has developed to its maximal possible extent, but I don't have that feeling. Everything I do—or I aspire to do—is still directed toward this greater purpose. The requirements of my daily physical existence must be secondary. The fact that no one would understand what I am talking about, should I commit the grievous error of confessing this purpose to anyone, has not diverted me from my goal.

Why do I strive to develop my soul when no one I know believes it exists? I cannot say that I really understand the reason. The stonemasons centuries ago voluntarily laying the foundations of the Cathedral of Notre Dame could not have known what would come of their labor, although they might have had some faint glimmerings of the architectural marvel that would arise.

They only knew they were laboring for a higher purpose. I have some faint glimmerings also. I imagine my soul to become a building block of some divine spiritual structure, perhaps even a keystone for some spiritual archway. I have been called upon to develop this soul of mine to its maximum potential. It is a *spiritual instinct* analogous to the instincts that drive migratory birds to fly over continents. I don't have to know why I have this instinct; I only am compelled to follow it to the best of my ability.

~ 5 ~

Following up on my earlier writings, I have been trying to reflect upon just how does one 'develop the soul'? It is not like building a house—or a cathedral—which are materialist endeavors. The spiritual effort of building one's soul has to be envisioned in metaphysical terms. What comes to mind are activities that give rise to a sense of the spiritual existence of the interior self—*meaningful* activities like thinking, learning, self-expression, vital experiences, creativity of every kind. A person knows when his soul is being developed. The basic supports of life—food, shelter, security—are necessary prerequisites for this effort. When these are unduly exaggerated or when they are totally lacking, the soul deteriorates. It is a tragic thing when a soul deteriorates, but it is all too common in human societies.

The more materialistically complex a society, the more development of one's soul becomes a difficult effort at which few are successful. As Spinoza says at the end of his *Ethics* on achieving the saving wisdom, "But all things excellent are as difficult as they are rare."

~ 6 ~

Salvation does not come from a 'savior,' it comes from the mystical spirit that every human being has the potential to possess. What is 'salvation' anyway? It is fulfilling the spiritual promise lying dormant in individuals, a promise that can only be grasped spiritually. A mystical spirit allows one to become conscious of a depth within oneself transcending daily material interests and activities. The metaphysical groundwork of existence is present in these depths, relating the individual to eternity. 'God' is the English-language nickname for the metaphysical groundwork. It is easier to say one has found God than to say one has discovered the metaphysical groundwork of existence. But the latter is more descriptive of what is often meant.

When a spiritual potential of an individual is not realized (as is usually the case), the person sooner or later loses his soul to the society in which he lives. This is a tragic event, since fulfilling one's spiritual potential is far more important than participating in society. Participation in society is a necessary stage in human development, but it must be surpassed for the greater goals of spiritual fulfillment—creating one's soul and relating it to God. These are more important goals than finding societal success. But even beyond finding these goals, individuals finding God is necessary for God Himself.

This last statement is a mysterious idea, arising from the depths of mystical thought. Only those who have come to it themselves can appreciate its significance. Very few have tried to express it with language. Perhaps the most lucid of those who have dared to do so was the Catholic priest Angelus Silesius:

> Ich weiss das ohne mich Gott nicht ein Nu kann leben,
> Werd' ich zu nicht, er muss von Not den Geist aufgeben.
>
> I know that without me, God cannot live one moment,
> If I come to naught, he must from need give up his spirit.

Somehow this philosopher-poet escaped the bonfires of the Church!

There are many today who scoff at the idea of God, however it is expressed. They are the same ones who scoff at the reality of souls. They have been brainwashed by *scientism* to think all reality is material in nature and can be understood scientifically. The menace of scientism looming over the human mind threatens everyone, even the most independent spirits. It is as great a danger to human culture as were the barbarian invasions during antiquity or the plagues in the medieval era. Scientism encases the soul in a rigid mental cast, preventing it from developing to its full potential.

Consciousness of metaphysical depth does not take the form of concepts expressed in language. It is rather a feeling, more akin to the feeling of *holiness* than that of understanding. This feeling may be generated in various ways—through ritual, architecture, music, art, reading. The book entitled *The Idea of the Holy* by Rudolf Otto explains the nature and meaning of holiness in an unmatched manner. It is up to individuals experiencing the sensation of holiness to generate appropriate concepts that can be communicated and can provide stability for these metaphysical feelings.

Nationalistic fervor is one of the main ways in which responsibility of an individual to develop his soul can be evaded. Appealing to 'patriotism' is one of the worst forms of harm that can be inflicted upon individuals. It is possible to support reasonable policies of one's country without falling into a soulless state of mind exemplified by the motto "my country, right or wrong." Development of one's soul comes ahead of development of one's country. The word 'country' itself is an abstraction and, like all abstractions, has only a limited degree of reality.

Nevertheless, many important personages have succumbed to the lure of nationalistic fervor. European nationalisms were responsible for the suicidal wars of Europe in the first half of the twentieth century. The figure of Adolf Hitler reveals the degree to which the sentiment of patriotism can dominate the minds of intelligent individuals. Hitler justified all his excesses in the name of the 'soul' of the German people. It did not seem to occur to him that there was no such thing. English and American nationalisms have been more colonial or economic in nature than homicidal, but in the long run have been just as harmful to individual spiritual development. Today the conceited American image of itself as leader of the 'free' world is doing immeasurable damage to itself and to other countries around the globe.

Even such a profound thinker as Nicholas Berdyaev fell into the trap of nationalism through his idealization of 'Holy Mother Russia.' He believed that after shaking free of

Communism, the Russian Christian spirit was destined to lead the world into a new era of spirituality (*Toward A New Epoch*, 1947). That this is not the case is clearly evident today in the policies of post-Communist Russia. Nationalism of whatever brand cannot substitute for reverence for one's own soul.

~ 7 ~

I have established to my own satisfaction that the wellbeing of my soul needs to be the principal focus of my life. However, a nagging feeling persists that a metaphysical soul cannot be a total isolate in the greater scheme of things, that there must be some metaphysical dimension of which it is a part and plays its role. I have tried to become conscious of this dimension but have been unsuccessful. No God has ever spoken to me nor have I become aware of any metaphysical 'groundwork' in which I exist. In all honesty, I must admit that terms from German mysticism like *Gottheit* or *Ungrund* have no existential meaning for me. It seems to me that the great theologian Paul Tillich's coy definition of the object of theology, "what concerns us ultimately" (*Systematic Theology*, Vol. 1), means that he is in the same situation as I am, that he has no existential experience of deity.

There are two choices here—either there is no object of ultimate concern (using Tillich's term) or I do not have the capacity to experience it. The latter is a real possibility since any mystical receptivity I might have had was probably lost during my long years of immersion in a scientific, materialist culture (this was true for Darwin, Freud, and no doubt many, many other outstanding thinkers). I am an empirical creature in that it is virtually impossible for me to genuinely grasp the existence of anything not founded on sensory experiences. Miraculously, I have become conscious of my own soul (grace?) but it may be that this achievement does not extend outside of myself. I am no mystic even though I believe that the capacity for mystical insight ought to be an essential quality of *Homo sapiens*. Others have possessed it. However, the metaphysical universe outside of myself seems to be beyond the limits of my consciousness. *C'est dommage!*

~ 8 ~

I am becoming conscious of a constant *longing* in the depths of my soul. The longing waxes and wanes but it is always there. It is like a gravitational force of which I am unaware but which is always affecting me. I find it difficult to say just what I am longing for; it is something unutterable, ineffable, beyond my power to describe. What I can confirm is the presence of a longing within me to reach out to something 'beyond'. Is it God for which I yearn? I cannot say; 'God' is just a word that carries no mystical connotation for me. If I were more mystically gifted, perhaps I could say more. But what I can say is that the longing is a powerful reality in me. It must have some significance, it must be telling me that there is something missing from my life, something I sorely need.

    What is to be done?

(Later....) When I die, I wonder if my soul will be released and fly to the source of this longing? The stronger my soul, the faster it should be able to fly to it. Then I will learn more about metaphysics. Meanwhile, the life I presently lead represents only the opportunity to develop my soul. I am aware of a certain affinity between my way of thinking and that of the medieval scholastics, whom I admire—except my 'faith in search of understanding' depends entirely on my own mind and does not require any *imprimatur* of official Roman Catholicism. I always think of Thomas Aquinas as his own self and not the 'Angelic Doctor' or 'Saint Thomas.' The idea of 'Thomism' I refuse to countenance and I think to be degrading to the memory of that remarkable thinker.

As an aside, one should remember that Aristotle did not know the term 'metaphysics'. It was a later editor of his writings who coined this status-lowering expression. For Aristotle, what is now called metaphysics was *Wisdom* or *First Philosophy* or, surprisingly even, *Theology*.

~ 9 ~

I like to read the Bible, especially the New Testament Greek scriptures with the side-by-side Koiné Greek and English. I read them often. But I form my own judgments about what they say. I have never understood why so much is made of love of one's fellow man in present day Christianity. It seems to me that the outstanding contribution of the Christian worldview has been its recognition of the role of *spirituality* in the human condition. Christian 'person love' (*agapé*) is a psychological state of mind far removed from spirituality. According to the gospel of Matthew, Jesus said the greatest commandment was to "love the Lord thy God with all thy heart and all thy soul and all thy mind" (Mt. 22:37). This doesn't leave much room for one's fellow man. The second commandment mentioned "to love thy neighbor as thyself" is clearly not on the same level of importance in Jesus' mind as the first. It comes from Leviticus as part of a detailed list of behavioral requirements that Israelites were expected to follow ('the law'). It seems to me that what was meant here was to treat your neighbor respectfully and not to take advantage of him. This of course only applied to fellow Israelites in biblical times.

Somehow the idea has gained credence in Christian religion that God *is* love, and therefore Christians must love all people, especially fellow Christians. The idea must have developed from the Gospel of John and particularly from his first Epistle where there is a constant emphasis on God's love for those who love him—that's not quite everyone! It is the gospel I like least of all. I suspect a very needy person or persons wrote it. It has given rise to the Christian obsession of basking in the love of Jesus. Whatever the case, the writings of John are dominated by Hellenistic concepts out of place in the teachings of a provincial Galilean rabbi, no matter how inspired he might have been. They could have been written by a philosopher from the Academy, or even by Plato himself.

Paul also in 1 Corinthians waxes eloquent on the necessity of *agapé*. But two Christian-dominated millennia after Jesus taught and Paul wrote, it is evident that the emotion of Christian personal love, as opposed to love of 'humanity', is rare among Christians; much more common are emotions of indifference, dislike, envy, contempt, and even hate. Dante is a more reliable guide to 'Christian' feelings than Paul. It has been said that continuation of a belief long proven to be untenable is a sign of mental illness. Myself, I think it quite admirable to genuinely love one's own soul, a difficult enough task in itself. If this is accomplished, one may move on to the more spiritually advanced state, which is the love of God, however one conceives of him. These accomplishments should be more than enough for any right-minded individual.

~ 10 ~

An Essay On Man by Ernst Cassirer (1944) represents in my mind the high point of European scholarly culture. Like many outstanding intellectual figures in Germany, he was forced to leave his country by Nazi anti-Jewish fanaticism. Cassirer draws upon the philosophical, literary, and scientific achievements of western civilization to express his view of the nature of the human condition. In the penultimate chapter, he clearly states his final position, "Science is the last step in men's mental development and it may be regarded as the highest and most characteristic attainment of human culture." Here, a century later, is a restatement, albeit in more elegant form, of Auguste Comte's theory of the three stages of development: religion, metaphysics, science—the last being the highest stage. Of course, Cassirer as a product of German *Bildung* is thinking of science as *Wissenschaft*, which is a more inclusive concept than the English term 'science'. *Wissenschaft* includes scholarly pursuits, while the English language term refers to empirical investigations. Yet in final analysis, both science and *Wissenschaft* refer to man's analytic approach to knowledge that leads to his comprehension and domination of his environment.

In spite of my admiration of Cassirer, I don't see science or *Wissenschaft* as the "highest and most characteristic attainment of human culture." Today, more than ever, science seems to be a dead-end street, culturally speaking, leading to ever more meaningless, absurd, and self-destructive activities. For me, the highest attainment of culture is a deepening consciousness of one's self, of one's soul, and its relationship to a metaphysical ground of existence (in a word, God), a goal that is generally ignored today. One may properly call this concept 'mysticism', even though the word is held in ill repute in contemporary intellectual circles. However, regardless of ill repute, the task of a relevant philosophy is the transmutation of mystical consciousness into coherent concepts that can enlighten the soul and be able to be transmitted to others. Then, as Alfred de Vigny said in his *Journal*, "*attrape qui peut.*"

Nicholas Berdyaev has asserted his feelings on this matter with his customary passionate depth of thought:

> The supreme values of an established culture are as indifferent to man's inner life, as cruelly disposed toward the human personality, as are the historical and natural worlds. This being so, culture also has its Day of Judgment—cultural idolatry is as reprehensible as barbarism. But there is no alternative: we have to face this tragic conflict, this insoluble antimony, and assume full responsibility for it. There is no alternative but to shoulder the burden of the terrifying, distressing and degraded world. Our only escape lies in the knowledge that there is an ultimate solution in the extra-natural sphere of Being, in which we participate also by virtue of our spiritual life.
>
> *Solitude and Society*, 1938, trans. George Reavey

I fear that I have not risen to the level of social and cultural responsibility advocated by Berdyaev and lived *to the hilt* up until the end of his life.

~ 11 ~

My thoughts are too *evanescent*. They need the physical embodiment of being written down on paper to achieve some stability for my future use.

~ 12 ~

The other day I walked with Amigo along an arroyo forming one of the deep ravines crisscrossing the National Forest. As I penetrated deeper into the forest, I felt as though entering a place where no white man had been before. The feeling of solitude was overpowering. Seated on a rock while watering Amigo, the familiar questions rose up in my mind—what have I done with my life? Why am I here? What should I do now? I fled society to escape the obsessions with money, the power struggles, the crass materialism, the search for demeaning pleasures; but with what have I replaced them? The idea of 'developing my soul'? Does this idea have any foundation in reality? Can I even be sure I have a soul to develop?

I find I must rework continuously in my mind that my soul does exist, that it is worthy of the sacrifice of societal gratifications, that my faith in its primacy is well founded and deserving of my total commitment. None of these ideas come naturally to me and require continual effort on my part to maintain them. I have intimations of a greater spiritual reality beyond my soul, but these are only intimations; justification of my way of life must rest on absolute *reverence* for my own soul.

It seems to me that my state of mind and way of life is most akin to the Greek Cynics of antiquity, even though they have never been viewed as metaphysical in their outlook on life. (The current meaning of the word 'cynic' is far removed from the Cynic movement of ancient Greece.) My 'bible' of Greek Cynicism is *Les Cyniques Grecs: Fragments et Témoignages* by Léonce Paquet. There is no equivalent English language source I know of which expresses as well the significance of Greek Cynicism and provides what is left of their thoughts. They wrestled with the problems of existence in the same way that I do. They asserted that the ultimate values of an individual should rest on independence of self, free expression of thought, questioning of established mores, escape from oppressive customs, cosmopolitan outlook, and return to nature. By nature, they did not mean a primitive world opposed to civilization, but an emphasis on the basic qualities of things, especially the qualities of human beings. They deplored a purely mental approach to philosophy; the total involvement of body and soul was practiced by them. They *lived* their philosophy. Finally, they placed no reliance on Gods who are beyond human reach. I say *Bravo!* to all of these ideas.

Contemporary academic philosophy does not regard the Greek Cynics as worthy of inclusion in the corpus of traditional philosophy. They left behind no system or technique to explain the nature of things. They are omitted from the usual philosophy textbooks. To my mind, however, they represent one of the most significant developments of philosophy, a development that will be remembered long after the analytical minutiae of modern philosophical scholarship will have crumbled into dust.

~ 13 ~

If I tell the occasional person I meet that I am a philosopher, they immediately get a fallacious idea about me. They think I am a professor who lectures students at a university and writes incomprehensible tracts on esoteric subjects unrelated to real life. They don't understand I am an *independent philosopher* outside of the academic world. However, for me, the distinction between academic philosophy and independent philosophy is a crucial one. The criterion for merit in the former is based on scholarship, for the latter it is based on creativity. Today, virtually all individuals who identify themselves as philosophers are academics dependent upon university credentials and publication lists. Independent philosophers like myself are rare.

It was not always so. The pioneer philosophers of ancient Greece were free spirits without institutional training wheels. It was their way of life that characterized them as philosophers. When they formed schools, it was the total package that attracted adherents. In fact, with the exception of Plato, writings of philosophers were usually summaries of their teachings—occasionally in metric form of dubious poetical merit—rather than literary products. (Plato was the first real litterateur of philosophy.) They freely philosophized as their spirit moved them, gave instruction, or formed schools. They often changed attachments to different teachers or locales. They supported themselves in diverse ways. By and large, philosophers lived ascetic lives that did not require much monetary income. The philosophical schools of Athens lasted for centuries and exerted a great influence on the intellectual life of the Greek cities and, later, on the Roman Empire. But when Christianity became the official religion of Rome and took hold of culture in the Empire with an iron grip, independent philosophy lost its vitality. It became, as the expression went, the handmaiden of religion. This lasted throughout the Middle Ages. But things changed when the Renaissance made its appearance in Europe. Philosophers seemed to be on the verge of acquiring a new vitality and a new independence in countries not dominated by the Catholic Inquisition, as was the case in Spain, Italy, and Portugal.

However, an unforeseen development took place, initially in Germany and then throughout Europe and the Americas. Philosophers were given a home in universities; they received salaries, titles, pensions, and the security of tenure. Human nature being what it is even for philosophers, they took to university life like ducks to water. In exchange, though, they lost their freedom—some might say their souls. When the scientific mindset reached the universities, philosophers had no means of defense. They were placed in departments and became scholars, historians, and lecturers to masses of immature students. Scholarship was the order of the day and to be successful, one had to excel as a scholar, i.e. a learned person with objectivity and critical thinking skills. These are the qualities necessary for academic or scientific success.

The difference between academic (university) philosophy and independent philosophy is immense. The former have paid secure positions. They have the prestige associated with professorial titles. In exchange, they must conform to the standards of scholarship that form the basis of the modern university. They must publish in peer-reviewed journals, write books for university presses, and be recognized as authoritative experts in some aspect of their profession. They must develop some skill in lecturing. If they perform successfully in these areas, they will receive the much-coveted lifetime tenure for their position. Independent philosophers have none of these rewards nor do they have the constraints. What they do have, however, is freedom to *express themselves* through philosophy, fully and unrestrictedly. This is an inestimable benefit since it promotes development of their souls.

The substance of 'scholarship' is founded on a scientific mindset where objectivity, precision, and comprehensive knowledge are essential elements in the progress of science. However, this mindset is almost always incompatible with creative philosophy where subjectivity and freedom must reign. There may be exceptions like Aristotle or Kant, but these are rare. For the most part, the dictum of Nietzsche holds true, *"Ein Gelehrter kann nie ein Philosoph warden,"* a scholar can never be a philosopher (*Schopenhauer as Educator*). The mental qualities needed for the two forms of thought are too disparate.

The brilliant essay by Nietzsche referred to above was published in 1874 when he was only 30 years of age. He was still professor of classical philology at the University of Zurich and had not yet entered into his remarkable life as an independent philosopher. It is amazing how much of what Nietzsche wrote more than a century ago about academia still rings true. One difference is that the State no longer makes decisions about the composition of university faculty; now each university department is a little fiefdom of its own, but the same conditions he described still hold true. The academic guild spirit based on traditional scholarship and antagonistic to creative independent thought is as strong as ever. It is upon the shoulders of independent philosophers that a future of philosophy will have to lie, if it is to have a vital future. So say I in this little polemic!

~ 14 ~

Insomniac Thoughts: In the middle of a sleepless night, it occurred to me that when I worked at the post office I had two lives, one at the sorting area of the post office, the other at the writing desk in my apartment. They were as separate from each other as the life of a royal prince of England is from a beggar boy in London's East End. When one of these lives weighed too heavily upon me, I could retreat in my mind to the other. Now, however, I have only one life and I have to concentrate all my energies upon it. Is it really an advance over the many factitious lives I have led in the past? Who cares what I do or think? Do I care myself? I eat and drink now but meagerly, and I no longer make merry at all. Perhaps the Greek sage was right in saying the only thing better than death is never to have been born. But if the ancient sage had not been born, how would that strangely calming thought have entered into my mind?

Reading again for the umpteenth time Pessoa's *Livro do Desassossego*, I come across a passage that I underlined years ago. He noted that immediately upon coming in contact with another person or persons, regardless of circumstances, all that was significant in his mental activity came to a standstill. A feeling of drowsiness began to overwhelm him, a situation that is all too familiar to me. It is only when he is alone that he is able to function creatively. "My way of life is in solitude, not amidst men"; Pessoa says that he quotes from either Rousseau or Senancour, he is not sure which one. And I too quote one of them at third hand because it tells me I am not completely alone in the annals of humanity. My choice of solitude is the right one for me.

~ 15 ~

Last evening, when I walked outside my cabin to sample the fragrance of the night air, I caught sight again of the mountain lion. He was at the spot where he had killed a deer some time ago, perhaps thinking he would find remains of the carcass. We looked at each other steadily for a moment. His square tawny head with leonine expressionless features had a hypnotic effect on me. I had the eerie sensation that behind those lion features was a spirit assessing me and relating to me. I had no fear, as there was something in his look that told me I was not in danger. If I could have, I would have stroked that tawny head, but I knew that was impossible. Suddenly the mountain lion retreated back into the forest. The moment was over.

I believe mountain lions are one of the noblest products of nature. Unlike most other animal species (including humans), they lead a solitary life except for brief mating periods. They range over many miles, supposedly in search of food, but perhaps also because of an exploratory instinct that biologists have not yet recognized. Mountain lions (pumas, cougars, panthers) have been exterminated over much of North America, especially in the United States, but they still live in wild areas like my Coronado National Forest.

If animals have souls, the mountain lion would surely have one of its superior forms. They are independent, brave, strong, noble creatures. They represent nature at its best in creating life forms. If transmigration of souls occurs, I would prefer my soul to be reborn as a mountain lion. Who is to say that a mountain lion with its qualities of character, strength, and ability to exist independently in the world is not dearer to God than human beings with all their language, cleverness, and destructive natures? Retribution will surely come to those who without reason and only for their own perverted pleasure destroy one of God's noblest creations.

~ 16 ~

Having reached a chronological age in which following each day, continuation of my life into the next is uncertain, each night I invoke this final thought, in case I do not see the light of the next day:

> "To the Creative Force far above me: I have said in my life what I have thought and done in it what I have been able. Now I bequeath my yearning soul to you for whatever you deem it to be worth."

~ 17 ~

Again, the sole purpose of my writing is the development of my soul. I look to generate wisdom for myself; any other consequence would be secondary. I aim toward achieving the *gnothi seauton* advocated by the Delphic oracle. Not just *knowing* but *becoming*. As an independent philosopher, I cannot allow myself to be distracted by the meaningless noise of analytic philosophy or the philosophical pretensions of certain biologists or theoretical physicists.

I am not a litterateur, one who is devoted to the cultivation of language. Nor have I any interest in the vast entertainment and instructional industries oriented toward markets. I am not like the medieval scholastics that worked toward a dogmatic system of belief. What I aim to do is develop my soul in an independent manner by whatever means are available to me. Unlike the vast majority of people today who do not take the existence of souls seriously, the spiritual excellence (arête) of my soul is the principal motivation for my efforts. The superiority of the Stoic philosophy, early and late, to that of today is based on the value they placed on the soul. Its development and protection guided all their activities. In my view, the abandonment of Stoicism's soul-based philosophy in favor of the Christian salvation-based religion has been greatly responsible for the spiritual ills of today.

My model figure in philosophy is Marcus Aurelius Antoninus, the Roman emperor from 161–180 A. D. He represents an outstanding example of the Stoic emphasis on cultivation of one's own soul, in spite of the vast responsibilities and power vested in him during his tenure as emperor. The thoughts of Marcus have fortunately come down to the contemporary era in his journal that later editors labeled *Meditations of Marcus Aurelius*. What is so remarkable about Marcus is that he was able to cultivate and express a personal spiritual philosophy, even while fulfilling his role as emperor of the greatest empire the world has ever known, stretching from the Atlantic to the Euphrates, from northern Europe to North Africa. Academics have tended to disparage him as a philosopher, saying that he was only an imitator of the original figures of Stoicism. He was not a litterateur like Seneca or a pedagogue like Epictetus. But he was personal and direct in his writing (in Koiné Greek). He had reverence for his own soul, which puts him head and shoulders above the scholarly pedants who have disparaged him.

It is not necessary to accept everything that Marcus wrote. His ideas about God and the State are not mine. The important thing about him was that he did not relinquish the primacy of his own soul in spite of the temptations that must have been offered him. He was able to express his spiritual feelings in a direct manner, without recourse to the prestige of his position. His high view of the human soul has inspired devoted readers throughout the centuries. Today, when the concept of soul has been relegated to the dustbin of superstition, he can point the way toward a renewal of spiritual consciousness.

As an aside, my scanty knowledge of ancient Greek (the language of Marcus' *Meditations*) suggests to me that it resembles in style—and even in content on occasion—the Koiné Greek of the synoptic Gospels. The emphasis on the wellbeing of the soul pervades both writings and the similarity of some of Marcus's thoughts to Jesus' teachings is quite remarkable. Perhaps early Christianity affected Marcus more than he was willing to admit.

~ 18 ~

When I make my rare excursions into the urban world, I find that people look upon me with suspicion. It may be the way I look, the way I dress, or that my isolated existence has rendered me unable to relate easily to strangers. They think I am some type of misfit, perhaps a mentally ill person. The most charitable view I have encountered is that I am approaching senility and there is no one to care for me. I have to put up with the humiliation of having no respect and no understanding by the society around me. It is not saying too much that leaving my solitary existence for the outside world is often a kind of torture that I must endure. Perhaps it is for the greater good of my soul. "What doesn't destroy me strengthens me." I can't remember who said that but I hope it is true. On the other hand, I am wondering if I should buy some new clothes, trim my beard, and spend a little more time in Tucson.

~ 19 ~

The Islamic fanatics who blow up marketplaces and mosques filled with innocent people reveal the dangers of an immoderate belief in God. Their suicide bombers die uttering their devotion to Allah. They are contemptuous of infidels who they say love life more than they love Allah. They say they love death when it carries out the will of their god.

It is not necessary to subscribe to the cruel dictates of Islamic fanatics to realize that there is more than a grain of truth in their judgments about western society. The people of western cultures, especially in the United States, do love life excessively. It is a wrong direction for the wellbeing of the soul. Death is part of life and its advent is not to be feared more than any other aspect of life. The attitude of the antique Stoics toward death is to be greatly recommended for the modern world. They maintained that no one knows the fate of the soul at the end of life; if it is dissolution, it is no great tragedy; if it is entry into a metaphysical dimension of existence, it may be an improvement over its terrestrial condition. I am inclined to believe the latter, but neither outcome warrants the lengths that people today go to in order to artificially extend their lives.

A person who surveys the architecture of today will see that the imposing cathedrals of yesteryear have given way to the imposing skyscrapers of business, and equally imposing temples for medical treatment. The former are more prominent, but the latter are more dangerous for the human soul. Scientism has resulted in the phenomenon of physicians replacing priests. I have decided that the latter are much to be preferred. The dignity and quality of human life is diminished by unnatural emphasis on its prolongation. It is sad to see elderly people whose age should have conferred wisdom upon them orient their lives according to the distance to their doctors' offices. These attitudes are reflected in the plight of the American economy where perpendicularly increasing medical expenses are on the verge of bankrupting the nation. There is no limit to the capacity of health industries to enrich themselves at the expense of the gullible American public. They prey upon the fear of disease and death that is so prevalent in American society. Worst of all, otherwise intelligent individuals become dependent on the dictates of an out of control medical establishment.

It is ultimately the exaggerated love of life that is responsible for their predicament. An intelligent philosophy of human life would permit individuals to live a life more appropriate for *Homo sapiens,* in which disease and death would not be feared more than hellfire and damnation. It is through metaphysical expansion of the mind that one can become free of these fears. In today's world, this can only come about through philosophy, real philosophy, not what now passes for such in the universities and their imitators.

~ 20 ~

The virtues of Stoic philosophy do not require that one become involved with the theoretical complexities of antique Stoicism that emerged during its almost one-thousand-year history. The traditional division of Stoic thought into Logic, Physics, and Ethics is irrelevant today. The Roman followers of Stoicism whose writings have largely survived were interested in its global aspects, since they themselves were usually political figures. What is important about Stoicism now (and during its initial flowering) is its focus on the *rationality* of the soul (ruling reason, mind, psyche) along with its spiritual qualities. This focus can be traced back to Socrates' acceptance of the Delphic dictum *gnothi seauton*, know one's self (γνωθι σεαυτον). The Stoics were devoted to the *wellbeing* of the soul, its excellence (arête), and never doubted its actual existence in some manner of being. Arguing about its nature, as Aristotle did, leads nowhere; the point is that it exists, not as a bodily organ, but as a metaphysical reality.

A thoughtful person has to resist the compulsive tendency to think in solely objective, material terms. This tendency must be based on some kind of primitive survival instincts. Goethe's comment given in the sarcastic utterance of Mephistopheles (Goethe's alter ego) in *Faust* is appropriate here:

> Daran erkenn ich den gelehrten Herrn!
> Was ihr nicht tastet, steht euch meilenfern,
> Was ihr nicht fasst, das fehlt euch, ganz und gar,
> Was ihr nicht rechnet, glaubt ihr, sei nicht wahr,
> Was ihr nicht wäge, hat für euch kein Gewicht,
> Was ihr nicht münzt, das, meint ihr, gelte nicht.
>
> Now I recognize the learned gentleman!
> What you can't touch, stands far removed from you,
> What you can't hold, for you does not exist,
> What you can't measure, you're sure can't be true,
> What you can't weigh, has no weight for you,
> What you don't coin, that, you think, is without worth.
>
> Faust, Part II, 1ˢᵗ Act (my translation)

None of the writings of Zeno, the founder of Greek Stoicism (ca. 300 B.C.) has survived the vicissitudes of antiquity, even though it was one of the most important philosophical movements of the times. The same is true of all the other important figures of the early Stoa. Modern readers are dependent upon the commentaries of Cicero (who presumably had them available to him) to learn about their content. The available writings of later Roman devotees of Stoicism (Seneca, Epictetus, Marcus Aurelius) contain the Roman versions of Stoic thought. Translators like George Long who immersed himself in the writings of Marcus are helpful commentators. Unfortunately, Long's insightful extensive introduction to Marcus' *Thoughts* is rarely provided with his translation. But there is really no substitute for reading the originals. Those lucky few—very few indeed, other than classical scholars who generally suffer with the personal limitations imposed by rigorous scholarship—those few who can read Greek (Epictetus, Marcus) and Latin (Cicero, Seneca) have an enormous advantage in grasping the outlook of Stoicism. This is the consequence of virtually eliminating classical languages from school curricula.

The resemblances of Stoic thought to early Christianity has been often noted. But Stoicism never carried the dogmatic baggage of Christianity. There was no such thing as 'heresy'. There was no incarnate God serving to save the faithful, no 'inspired writings' containing his will. The Stoics studied the teachings of their eminent philosophers; they did not deify them. This makes Stoic thought far more attractive to independent, educated individuals. And so it has been throughout European and American history of philosophy, up to and including the scholarly Professor Ernst Cassirer in his last two books (*An Essay on Man* and *The Myth of the State*).

It has been said that Christianity displaced Stoicism in the course of antiquity because the former met human needs not fulfilled by the austere Stoic code of living. This may well be true, although the bizarre imposition of Christianity on the Roman Empire by the Emperor Constantine must have also played a role. Faith in a savior trumped rational thought. It is a sad commentary on the human condition that psychology trumps intellectuality. To imagine otherwise has probably been a naïve tendency on my part.

The most important writers of Roman Stoicism—Cicero, Seneca, and Marcus Aurelius—have been an essential element in my survival as an independent philosopher. I have learned to ignore disparaging critiques of these towering figures of antique philosophy by scholarly pedants. Their books occupy the few functional shelves in my library, along with Emerson, Thoreau, Nietzsche, Pessoa, and Berdyaev.

~ 21 ~

Along with the soul, antique Stoicism, especially in the Roman era, emphasized the social nature of human beings and the importance of fellowship. The term 'love of neighbor' is even used by Marcus Aurelius to advocate concern for others. The resemblance to Christian ethics is striking. Solitude is rejected as a means of coping with the problems of society. I have to admit I have not followed these tenets of Stoicism. I want as little to do as possible with my fellow man who usually repels me; thus solitude has held a great attraction for me. But still I wonder if I possess a personality defect that impels me to reject society.

It seems to me on reflection, however, that the world I live in is so far removed from the Stoic world of antiquity that the recommendations of Stoic philosophers cannot be applied today. Society presses in now far more strongly on the individual than it ever did in antiquity. There may be more security but there is less freedom. The individual is hedged around on all sides by the pressures of the media, of the advertising industries, of government bureaucracy, of intrusive commerce, of the increasing complexity of every aspect of societal life. Emerson's judgment that "things are in the saddle and ride mankind" is truer now than he ever could have imagined. In sheer population density, the world is pushing past seven billion people, while the Roman Empire in its largest extent has been estimated at no more than fifty million. The comparison is just because the communication industries have made the entire contemporary world 'neighbors'; today we quickly know more what is happening in the mountains of Nepal than the Romans knew about events a hundred miles away in Naples. For all these reasons, the need for solitude, for separation, is greater, at least for me than ever before. *Radical solitude* has been necessary for my sanity and my development.

~ 22 ~

I am reading Fr. S. Janos' translation of *The Philosophy of Inequality* by Berdyaev. It is one of my favorite books of his and has not been available to English readers until now. I like its angry tone and political incorrectness. The chapters on 'Socialism' and 'Culture' are particularly interesting. But Berdyaev cannot rid himself of his idolatry of Jesus Christ and his hanging on to Christianity—I don't know why. If all culture and religion are symbolic, as he maintains, surely the idea of God incarnate in Christ falls into the same category. It is a weakness of Berdyaev's otherwise profound worldview.

~ 23 ~

On clear moonlit nights, I sometimes walk up to the ridge behind my cabin and contemplate the universe. The panorama of the glittering stars and the vast sky is spread out before my eyes. Occasionally, I can follow a shooting star making its way across the heavens. The gray mountains of Mexico loom up in the distance. I think what an insignificant speck I am in the enormity of the universe. Pascal, Kant, and Emerson at times felt the same way. Why do I take myself so seriously? The world was here before I arrived and will be so after I depart. The admonition of Boccaccio, "Eat, drink, and be merry, for tomorrow we die" comes to my mind.

Then I remember it is only my physical self that is this insignificant speck; my *soul*, oh yes, my soul! is something else. My soul is large and spacious, with many chambers, larger than any other entity of which I am aware. I have no knowledge of the dimensions of Deity, but I feel comparable to Him. Perhaps I am a Deity. The fact that I capitalize the word 'Deity" and I capitalize 'I' has a meaning. Why should Deity be limited to a single unity apart from souls? Why is not every expanded soul a manifestation of Deity? This is not pantheism, this is a type of *panentheism* without the cumbersome terminology of Karl Christian Krause and with concentration on the indwelling human Soul instead of a distant Deity. The physical world is plural; why should not a metaphysical Deity be plural as well? How much richer an existence would Deity have as plural instead of monadic!

I like to think of myself as an aspect of Deity. It gives me more self-respect than I might otherwise have. It gives a foundation to the doctrine preached by Nietzsche of 'reverence for self,' even if, unfortunately, he could not maintain it for his own self. Philosophers are no longer burned on a stake for such thoughts. But at least, in former times, a philosopher's thoughts were taken seriously which was why they might be exiled, tortured, or burned. Today no one cares or even notices what a philosopher thinks. If souls do not exist, what anyone thinks about such dubious entities does not seem to be worth wasting good wood upon.

At my age, I would prefer to quickly depart this life asphyxiated over a fire for my ideas, instead of stuck on a hospital bed, with tubing plunged into my blood vessels and orifices, and soulless physicians plying me with toxic drugs. It is too bad the authorities would not permit me to arrange a dignified *auto-da-fé*.

~ 24 ~

I don't vote in American national elections. I haven't voted for many years. There are those who think that not voting is antipatriotic, selfish, irresponsible, a sign of lack of concern for the nation. But for me, voting in a country with 340 million people is quite meaningless. My individual vote doesn't count for anything. And even if it did, I wouldn't have any idea for whom I was voting. I never know any candidates personally. All I know is the image created by the vast propaganda machines that are behind every candidate, if they are to have a chance of being elected. Nothing they say can be believed; everything they claim to stand for is a farce, only designed to persuade voters to vote for them. In a nation the size of the United States, politics is necessarily demagoguery. If I were to vote, it would be a complete abandonment of my self-respect as an honest individual.

It is said that democracy began in the city-states of ancient Greece. There most people had some direct knowledge of political figures. I think it was Aristotle who was quite firm on his belief that city-states should not exceed a maximum population. If the population exceeded a certain figure (I don't recall what it was but I think well under 100,000), surplus individuals should emigrate. That is how cities were started all over the Mediterranean shores by emigrating Greeks. What would Aristotle say about the American empire of 340 million and constantly increasing?

Since there is rarely any personal knowledge of candidates in huge countries, politicians strive to create government dependency situations where people vote for those who they think will best serve their own interests. For example, everyone knows that the senior citizens of America (fast becoming the majority) will vote for politicians who they think will maintain and expand free medical care for those 65 years of age and over, even though it is driving the country into economic ruin. This is a fundamentally flawed situation for a democracy in which the leaders are supposed to have the interests of the whole nation and its future as their priority. I could go on and on. But this is why I don't vote. It would be a tacit endorsement of an irretrievably corrupt state of affairs.

The smaller a country, the better democracy works. This principle rules out its effectiveness in the large empires of the world: China, India, United States, Brazil, Indonesia, Russia, Mexico. Great empires, unlike peoples and languages, do not survive indefinitely; they disintegrate due to a law of entropy applied to empires. No small country wants to become part of a larger one, except under special circumstances as when independent Texas became part of the United States because they feared Mexico would regain possession of it. At the present time, every empire strives to be 'democratic,' just as they strive to increase their gross national product and keep everyone alive for the longest possible time. "What would you have?" an interlocutor might say to me, "dictatorship, theocracy, anarchy, no government at all?" No, I accept the government under which I live, much as I accept acts of nature—earthquakes, floods, hurricanes, drought—sometimes these are beneficial, usually not. I can't control the natural world, nor would I want to. I can only deal with it as best I can. But I don't have to vote since not voting in the United States is not yet a criminal offense.

~ 25 ~

It is true that at certain times, *ennui* tends to overcome me. I become restless, bored, anxious; I feel the need for something to draw me out of myself. At such times, I wonder about going to a big city—Tucson, Phoenix, New York—anywhere that will provide me with diversions, even though I know they will eventually only cause more ennui in my soul. Sooner or later, I turn to my most important resource for these times—Antisthenes' concept of the "storehouse of the soul." I found it in his speech given in Xenophon's essay *Banquet* describing an historical event in Periclean Athens. (Plato's account of the same banquet under the name of *Symposium* does not mention it, probably because Plato did not like Antisthenes.) In Xenophon's account, Antisthenes describes all the desires that trouble men, which he deals with by drawing upon his *storehouse of the soul* (της ψυχης ταμιευομαι) containing the wealth of philosophic knowledge he acquired from being in the company of Socrates. Furthermore, he says, this spiritual wealth has the additional advantage of providing him the leisure, untroubled by his former business worries, to go to whatever is worth seeing and hearing, and especially, to pass the whole day in the company of Socrates and absorbing his teachings.

I do not have the live example of a Socrates to provide me with spiritual wealth. I have to rely on my own initiative and resources. The solution to sexual appetite recommended by Antisthenes, which I have refrained from describing, does not work for me. But I have managed to put much wealth in the storehouse of my soul, even though I hope there is yet room for more. I draw upon it at times of ennui, much like people draw upon stores of food in times of famine. This wealth has never failed me. I know, of course, that Xenophon wrote *Banquet* many years after the actual event in Athens. One cannot expect complete historical accuracy, no more than the Gospels can provide exact historical accuracy of the life of Jesus. But by reading it, one can experience the Attic genius for philosophy that shines forth from *Banquet* and add to the storehouse of one's own soul, described so eloquently by Xenophon.

~ 26 ~

I have written before that I like to walk in the Coronado National Forest. It's worth repeating my experiences there because they form a major part of my life. The forest in my area is virgin with only deer paths. What I like to do is follow the arroyos that run through it. These are very desolate pathways and sometimes I think no one has ever been there before me. The arroyos are usually dry, but sometimes, during the summer monsoon season, they suddenly fill with water and become raging torrents where a person could drown. Once in a while, I have been caught in an arroyo during a rainstorm, requiring my clambering up the steep walls that often line it.

It is not easy walking along the arroyos. Amigo doesn't like them. Their floors are usually filled with stones—often great boulders that have been brought there by torrents of water, widening and deepening their beds. It is hard for me to imagine the torrents that must have been required to form these arroyos and bring down the boulders. Untold years must have been required to form these channels. And here I am, occupying only a speck of time during the hundreds of millennia that these arroyos have existed. My insignificance in time, the insignificance of all human life in time, is astounding. Like my insignificance in space, my insignificance in time cannot be exaggerated. How can anyone take the human phenomenon too seriously? We have appeared and will disappear in the flicker of a cosmic eyelash. All our comings and goings are like the buzzing of bees in their hive, which will stop immediately as soon as some event of nature destroys it. Paraphrasing the poet, the only sensible way to live is to eat, drink, copulate, and make merry.

These thoughts, however, depress me. I am not made to follow the advice of the poet. I have a longing to immerse myself in a *metaphysical* dimension of existence. Theologians might say I have a longing for God. Perhaps so, but as soon as I try to experience God in any way, he disappears. I have thought about the Greek myth of Orpheus and Eurydice. Orpheus by dint of his wonderful skill with the lyre charms the gods who allow him to rescue his beloved dead wife Eurydice from Hades. The one condition of the rescue was that Orpheus not look back at her until they have regained the world of the living. But Orpheus could not stand to wait; he turned to look at his beloved wife and she was thrust back to Hades, never to return. So it is with God and me; whenever I try to see him, he disappears. I have to be content with my longing without it ever coming to fruition. Perhaps if it did, I would die.

There is a flaw in the materialist logic about the insignificance of human beings. The flaw is that human existence is only material in nature, with a minute brief existence in the space-time dimensions. But there is as well a metaphysical dimension of human existence. Reverence for self is impossible without consciousness of this metaphysical dimension, without some awareness of the dualism that pervades human life. Rejecting dualism because of dogmatic monism is a grave error to which most unthinkingly subscribe at the present time. The metaphysical dimension is the one in which souls exist.

These are issues that should occupy the minds of thoughtful individuals and not be left to theologians, scientists, or mathematicians. Every serious person should work out his or her own worldview. The future of their souls may depend upon it.

~ 27 ~

Why is there no consciousness of the metaphysical dimension of existence in America? It seems to be limited to 'New Agers' who are usually lacking historical consciousness (an absolute necessity for intelligent metaphysics) and where the commercial and the metaphysical are inseparably mixed together. There is a fine book by Rudolf Otto published in the early 1920s and translated into English as *The Idea of the Holy* (*Das Heilige*). In it, the author describes and evaluates metaphysical longing in a scholarly manner. He expresses this longing as the *numinous* and attributes it to consciousness of a divine presence. Today in America, this book has no more general interest than a book on the extinction of the woolly mastodon. Its interest seems to be confined to Protestant seminaries.

After much cogitation on the subject, I have concluded that the lack of interest in the metaphysical dimension is to be attributed to the Christian religion. Unlike Nietzsche, I don't hate Christianity; I merely believe it has the demise of an intelligent metaphysics on its conscience. The awareness of a Divinity has been adulterated by the requirement of faith in Jesus, the Galilean rabbi, as His incarnation on Earth. In Christianity, one must believe that Jesus Christ did not merely possess divine attributes, but that one's own salvation can only come through belief in this incarnation. If one doesn't have this faith, then his soul is destined to come to a bad end.

This is idolatry on a grand scale. I share the aversion of the ancient Hebrews to idolatry in any form. Idolizing a dead personality is worse to me than idolizing a painted totem or a carved statue. It degrades the awareness of the 'numinous' for individuals. Christian dogmas have given a bad name to metaphysics for intelligent individuals and, in my judgment, are largely responsible for the dominance of scientism in the modern world. It is like the dog in the manger who is not able to feed on what is there, but keeps all other animals out.

Many of the eminent people in philosophy whom I admire have maintained their allegiance to Christianity (Feuerbach, Thoreau, and Nietzsche are exceptions). Who knows what philosophers like Kierkegaard, Berdyaev, and Tillich might have further accomplished if they had not been shackled to a superannuated religion. Who knows what Rudolf Otto himself might have accomplished if he had not been bound to the Chair of Theology at Marburg University. I do believe that until this incubus is removed from the backs of spiritually gifted individuals, the spirituality of the 'Christian' world is fated to be overwhelmed by a dominant scientism.

These writings I produce are not like any other of which I am aware. They are not a diary of events in my life, they are not literary memoirs, they are not a journal like that of Thoreau, recording his daily observations of nature, and they are certainly not confessions. I have nothing to confess. What they are, I believe, are *catalysts* for my metaphysical development. They may not have started that way, but that is what they have become. If this development should end, I would write no more.

Writing for me is a reciprocal process. I write down what is in my mind, but also the act of writing forms my mind, my soul, which latter is my mind viewed from a different angle. When I reread what I have written, I solidify what has been formed. Creative writing is a remarkable activity, marvelously suited for me. It has taught me to become what I am capable of becoming.

I sense that this is now the *kairos* in my life—the right time, the destined moment for me. Never mind that I have been living a solitary life for decades, never mind that I am approaching octogenarian status, never mind that no one knows me. Now is the *kairos,* the appointed time when all has come together to create my soul. Now I become what I have always wanted to become, a mainly spiritual human being—independent, conscious of the divine element, prepared for my existence here, or for a new existence elsewhere.

~ 28 ~

There is a type of madness that occurs when one has exhausted the possibilities of his earthly life and desires to withdraw his soul from it. This is not a dishonorable action and is a temptation for superior individuals, especially for philosophers. Friedrich Nietzsche is a prime example of such a withdrawal—and of its risks. One should not be frightened by madness. I will give the insightful words of Plato on the subject:

> And therefore it is just that only the mind of the philosopher has wings, for he is always, so far as he is able, in communion through memory with those things that cause God to be divine. Now a man who employs such memories rightly is always being initiated into perfect mysteries and he alone becomes truly perfect; but since he separates himself from human interests and turns his attention to the divine, he is rebuked by the masses who consider him mad [παρακινων—out of one's senses; lit. beside oneself] and do not know that he is inspired.
>
> *Phaedrus* (trans. Harold Fowler)

~ 29 ~

Some time ago, during my occasional visits to *The Book Stop* in Tucson, I came across an Italian book *La Solitudine dell'anima* (2011) by a psychiatrist named Eugenio Borgna. I have picked up enough Italian in past years to be able to read it. It contains many quotations and discussions from philosophers, poets, and, of course, psychiatrists (these categories do not belong together!). However, there was not a word I could find about the status of the term *anima* (soul). The author does not acknowledge its lack of currency in the modern world, especially the psychoanalytic world originated by Freud. What is the point of addressing the soul's solitude if scientific professions do not think it exists? No doubt Borgna thinks so himself as well, if he were pressed on the issue. No doubt he would say he was using the term metaphorically. But really, he was probably capitalizing on the literary panache of the term.

Apart from this lacuna, Borgna's book is an interesting compendium of opinions of famous writers, as well as his own, on the significance of solitude for mental health and mental illness. I found especially interesting his focus on the conceptions of solitude of Emily Dickinson in her poetry, although her poems sound strange in Italian. There can be little doubt that Emily Dickinson did believe in the existence of her soul.

In fact, it is my opinion that there is no condition other than solitude to be truly beneficial for the soul. Significant contact of souls with other souls is almost always wishful thinking made necessary by unawareness of a greater metaphysical reality to which one's own soul should relate. Truly, I believe, we are all metaphysical monads. In Martin Buber's language, *Ich–Es* (I–It) is the only reality in a material world. *Ich–Du*, (I–Thou) is an illusion, *except* where God is concerned. However, the word 'God' in the mouths of people today has become meaningless.

The meeting with an ultimate metaphysical reality on this side of the grave is a prospect much to be desired. I know that I do yearn for it. It is in medical terms the 'cure' for solitude. But for me, with my upbringing and background, I fear it can only be a yearning. Still, I think my yearning is better than the world's reality.

~ 30 ~

The Christian Gospels and Judaism. I have hesitated to commit to print my opinions on this subject for many years, even though I have devoted a great deal of thought to it. I am referring to the relationship of the historical Jesus to contemporary Judaism. One may think who am I, Leon Landesman, a person who has not set foot in a synagogue since his bar mitzvah at thirteen years of age and is in no way a trained biblical scholar, to discourse on the role of Jesus in 'Judaism'. But I cannot help it. I must write down what I think. I was born a Jew but have been attracted to the Gospels since childhood, even though in my otherwise secular family, the name Jesus on one's lips was implicitly forbidden and the New Testament a nonexistent writing. But I gained access, I cannot remember how, to a Christian Bible. The impact on me of the words of Jesus was a revelation. I think it was my first introduction to the meaning of spirituality.

Since then I have read the New Testament many times in many different versions. I have an interlinear Greek-English version that has been the means of my learning the Koiné Greek, not a recognized instructional device, but one that worked for me. (I should admit that I have looked into *New Testament Greek* by D. F. Hudson for some grammar and have as reference *Analytical Greek Lexicon* for the New Testament Greek Scriptures.) Right from the beginning of my interest, I noticed there is hardly a thought of Jesus that does not derive from the Hebrew Scriptures, principally the Pentateuch, Psalms, and Prophets. Any properly annotated version of the Greek Gospels will confirm this statement. Fortunately, I had enough childhood familiarity with the Hebrew Bible to recognize the relationship.

What is unique for me in the sayings of Jesus was his ability to bring to life the significant Old Testament thoughts and to convey a feeling of inspired spirituality to them that is for me quite remarkable. I am not going to try to give any examples because they must be *experienced* in context to get their full meaning. Jesus was a great symbolist, as Nietzsche once noted. The latter never directly attacked Jesus in his writings, only those who used him to found the cult of Christianity.

I have developed the conviction that Jesus was the greatest Jewish prophet and the culmination of a long line of prophets before him. It makes no difference that a Jewish Sanhedrin urged his crucifixion; this confirmed his breaking new ground for Judaism. Jewish prophets before him were done away with by Jewish kings and priests who felt threatened by them. Isaiah is said to have been sawed in half, Jeremiah barely escaped from a cistern where he had been thrown to die, others were stoned. Jesus himself mentioned that Jerusalem was the place where prophets were murdered and where he expected his own death. Almost all the prophets claimed that God spoke to them personally, in one way or another. Jewish exegetes and scribes ultimately recognized the significance of prophetic writings and caused the most important of them to be included in the canon of Hebrew Scriptures. But this did not happen in the case of Jesus.

Why has Jesus, the Galilean rabbi and prophet, been left out of the canon of the Hebrew Scriptures? No one denies he was a circumcised Jew brought up in Jewish traditions, that he preached to Jews in synagogues, that all his disciples were Jews, that his teachings were filled with references to Jewish Scripture, that the evangelists were Jews (Luke may have been a Jewish convert), that Paul, the apostle to the Gentiles, was a learned Jew. If there is anyone who deserves a central place in inspired Judaism, it is Jesus of Nazareth from Galilee. Yet Jews want nothing to do with him. One of the most important contemporary Jewish writings on the Biblical prophets, *The Prophets,* by Abraham Joshua Heschel, does not mention his name. Intellectual Jewish scholars and rabbis recognize Jesus' position in Christianity, but keep him at arm's length from Judaism. He is a nonexistent person in the chronicles of the Jewish religion. The scholarly and rabbinical community of Judaism is responsible for this yawning gap in Jewish religious thought.

There are, of course, reasons for this state of affairs. The uncritical worship of Jesus by his uneducated disciples offended the sensibilities of the strictly monotheistic Jewish priests and learned class. The latter did not distinguish between Jesus the spiritual teacher and prophet, and what his devoted admirers ultimately claimed him to be. They thought it unmitigated idolatry to claim him to be God incarnate. (Lower class Jews seem to this day to be prone to idolize their leaders. I have to confess that *Acts* seems to me to be the chronicles of an ongoing collective mania led by Peter and fanned by Paul.) What started as a Jewish sect had become an esoteric form of idolatry. Thus it is not surprising that the leaders of Judaism allowed Jesus to be absconded from their religion and excluded his thoughts from Hebrew Scriptures. The sayings of the Galilean rabbi were not even included in the rabbinical writings that developed after destruction of the Second Temple. Traditional Jewish leaders refused to acknowledge the remarkable spiritual contributions of Jesus to their own religion. An equally important reason, perhaps, was that there had been no scriptural prophets recognized for centuries. The canon for prophets in the Hebrew Bible had been rigidly established shortly after the return to Jerusalem from the Babylonian exile. There were to be no more. The inspired apocryphal writing *The Book of Wisdom* written in Greek by an Alexandrian Jew was also left out. (St. Jerome included it in the Latin Vulgate.) All these discussions are explanations but not justification for the rabbinical disavowal of the prophet Jesus of Nazareth.

Jesus had been unfortunate in his choice of disciples; none of the poorly lettered Galilean disciples wrote anything containing his original words that survived as literature. Matthew, the tax collector, may have written down some of his sayings, which were then translated into Greek, serving as source material for the Gospels. But Jesus had no Baruch, amanuensis for the prophet Jeremiah, to provide a definitive writing for him. He certainly had no Boswell or Eckermann. The devoutly religious Palestinian rabbis and Talmudists who decided about the traditional canons were probably not fluent in written Greek; the Greek 'Gospels' recounting the translated sayings of Jesus fell outside their realm, never mind their association with the Christian idolization of him. (Neither did the pious Ben Sirach nor the bicultural Philo Judaeus, a contemporary of Jesus, make it to the canon. Centuries later, the anti-Catholic Protestant leaders went along with the Hebrew canon; thus neither *The Book of Wisdom* nor *Ben Sirach* are to be found in Protestant Bibles, except occasionally as Apocryphal writings.) But whatever the reasons, there can be no valid excuse for excluding a great spiritual figure like Jesus, the Galilean rabbi, from the religious literature of Judaism.

Once the new religion of Christianity became the state religion of the Roman Empire, the situation changed drastically. Most Christians were by then of pagan origin and did not want to know anything about the Son of God being a Jewish rabbi. It became dangerous for Jews to talk about Jesus. Jews became labeled as Christ-killers and the object of mob hatred. This situation worsened throughout the Middle Ages and has persisted well into modern times. It would have been a brave but foolish Jew to publically claim Jesus as one of his own. To this day, in spite of the heritage of the Enlightenment and of religious eclecticism, Jews are *viscerally* regarded by many Christians with contempt and distaste. Nevertheless, regardless of Christian attitudes, I think it is high time for Jewish leaders to incorporate one of their own, one of their greatest prophets, into their religion. (The movement called 'Jews for Jesus' is merely a device for converting Jews to Christianity and has nothing to do with the importance of the human Jesus of Nazareth for Judaism.) The absence of the spirit of the Nazarene from Jewish religious thought might be one reason why I never participated in organized Judaism. This ends my long personal discourse on Jesus and Judaism.

~ 31 ~

> Das Werdende, das ewig wirkt und lebt,
> Unfass euch mit der Liebe holden Schranken,
> Und was in schwankender Erscheinung schwebt,
> Befestigt mit dauernden Gedanken!

This quotation from the Prologue to Goethe's *Faust* has always been an inspiration to me, which I feel has caught the spirit of philosophical creativity. Schain in *Affirmations of Reality* (1982) provides a poetical English translation:

> New creation, eternally occurring,
> Ye shall contain with love's kind attention,
> And what freely floats, dimly swaying,
> Surely shall you fix with lasting conceptions!

The work by Schain mentioned above focused on the philosopher expressing himself in a way that would affect others. My perspective is different: I think that the philosopher expresses himself in a way that will form his *own* soul. More personally and succinctly, *my writing has made me what I am.* The objectification of my thoughts in the written word somehow has molded my soul to become what it is now. If I had not formulated them as *dauernden Gedanken* and put them in written form, I would be a different person. This is a radical statement but I feel its truth deeply.

Why should this be so? The question has occupied my mind for many years, but I have never been able to answer it to my satisfaction. I can only conceive that there is something about the transmutation of one's feelings into linguistic form and the *fixing* them by means of the written word that alters the interior self, one's soul. A complex soul-mind alteration must occur. The writing may affect others but its profoundest effect is on one's own self. In his discussion of 'objectification', Berdyaev quotes with approval the mystic Russian poet Tyutchev, "A thought once spoken is a lie." Berdyaev says this is why he is never satisfied with his own writings. But if one reaches the desired state of reverence for his own soul, writing for himself is enough; one is not required to have the uncertain task of communicating with others. An abbreviated formulation is that the creative act makes the man—and perhaps alters God as well!

Authentic philosophers write out their philosophy. I believe this dictum universally holds true. The deepest motivation for philosophers—beyond the venal motives inevitably encountered in any society—is to form their own souls, consciously or unconsciously. Like all dictums, there are exceptions. The most notorious exception, of course, was Socrates. It is generally accepted that he wrote nothing. Instead, he was a famous talker. His talking has come down to modern times through Plato and Xenophon. Diogenes Laertius tells of the rumors that Socrates played a role in the composition of the plays of Euripides, but this has not been substantiated.

Socrates said that he was in search of "truth' in the dialogues he would conduct with whoever would listen to him. But beyond that, he was a great believer in his efforts to become the 'best' that he could, a belief that is clearly set forth in the last pages of Xenophon's *Memorabilia*. (In my opinion, Xenophon is a better guide to the real Socrates than is Plato.) There can be no doubt that Socrates felt he was accomplishing his improvement by discoursing with individuals who had a taste for philosophy. For some reason, he never turned to writing down his thoughts himself. However, the similarity of the effects of his talking to the writing of most philosophers is quite evident to me.

I am no neurologist but I am aware that the language localizations in the brain for speech and for writing are closely related. The brain is the receptive and executive organ for the soul, the place where the soul mysteriously interacts with its physical environment (a concept I hold). It is not surprising to me that speaking and writing, at a certain level, have similar effects on one's soul. Fortunately, not being a scientist held back from creative thought, I can freely speak my mind about these important metaphysical subjects.

~ 32 ~

I have felt a special affinity with two different individuals in the annals of philosophy, Friedrich Nietzsche (1844–1900) and Diogenes of Sinope (ca. 404–323 B.C.). Nietzsche's writings resonate with me. He was the quintessential *á rebours* personality. My circumstances are similar to what his were in many ways. I consider myself to be an independent philosopher but what I really am is an *isolated* philosopher, which was Nietzsche's situation as well. There is no one with whom I am personally intimate, as was the case with him. Both of us became utterly disconnected from our societies and became contemptuous of them. We abandoned academia. Unlike Nietzsche, I speak the language of the area I live in, but it does me no good since I rarely meet anyone with whom I can have a significant discussion. We both have lived on meager pensions; his was about to diminish when he lost his mind; mine may do so in the future since a question has arisen about my social security income. I am much older than he was during his writing prime, but I am in reasonably good health, which was not the case with him. With perhaps one exception, no literary person took his writing seriously until after his mental collapse. It is one of the greatest ironies of fate that after Nietzsche could no longer mentally function, he became world famous and his books are everywhere. I have not had a mental collapse, but even if I did it would probably not change the obscurity in which I live. But all in all, our similarities are great.

But...there is one great difference between us. Nietzsche gave in to the temptation to lapse into madness, a temptation he occasionally mentions in his writings. (See Schain's *The Legend of Nietzsche's Syphilis*.) I do not intend to give in to this temptation. I intend to *hold out*. My model in this regard is not Nietzsche but the ancient Greek Cynics, epitomized by the figure of Diogenes of

Sinope. Diogenes held out during his long life even though the pressures on him must have been greater than those on Nietzsche—or on myself. I am determined to stand my ground and make no concessions to what I regard as a decadent society. Diogenes lived in cities amidst people, whereas I live in the forest amidst animals, but there is no essential difference in the worldviews that we developed. Frankness of speech (παρρησια) for him translates into frankness in writing for me. Like Nietzsche, we both became free to live out our opinions in our ways of life.

Given his remoteness in antiquity, it is not surprising there is little reliable information about Diogenes. He lived a long life and must have had different periods in which his circumstances varied. Sometimes he lived on the streets, most famously in a barrel. He is said to have been a tutor of children, had a circle of followers, and to have been an author of a number of books, one of which, *Republic,* was praised by the noted Stoic philosopher, Cleanthes. None of his writings have survived. He was highly regarded by many in Athens and Corinth, and upon his death, statues were raised in commemoration of him. He was an extreme individualist, despising wealth, fame, and high birth. His skill at repartee was legendary. Like his predecessors, Socrates and Antisthenes, he valued philosophy above all else.

As a consequence of his way of life, Diogenes valued strength of mind more than any other virtues. His hero was Hercules, the mythical strong man of antiquity. He despised individuals who knew better, but went along with society out of weakness, fear, or doubt. One of his favorite targets, according to Diogenes Laertius, was Plato for whom he had little respect, since he felt the latter fawned on the rich and powerful. He disdained the ordinary conventions of society, which led Plato to characterize him as "a Socrates gone mad." But Plato did not have the character that would permit him to appreciate Diogenes. After all, Plato was fundamentally a litterateur, albeit a philosophically gifted one.

The academic world has almost uniformly dismissed Diogenes and his circle as authentic philosophers. Diogenes himself is regarded as a comical figure of antiquity, worthy of a place in a play of Aristophanes. Doubtless, this is because the image of a philosopher is very different for contemporary academicians than it was in the antique world. A tenured university professor with a comfortable income living a luxurious life is incapable of identifying with Diogenes, "the hound of heaven." For the Greek Cynics, it was an illusion to think that a mental life alone could make a philosopher. One had to boldly *live* according to his philosophy. Independence from social conventions, simplicity of living, and unrestricted freedom of speech were the essential qualities for a philosopher. These qualities cannot be found in the academic philosophers of today.

A hypothetical questioner criticizes me—who am I, a failed academician, a recluse living in a forest, a writer without readers—who am I to make such sweeping condemnations of my society! My answer is—I am who I am, I feel what I must, I think what my feelings tell me to think, and I freely write what I think. A place has been assigned to me in this world as I am; others can find their own place in it. The larger scheme of things is beyond my ken; I believe this is as it should be, given my microscopic dimensions. I have no wish to know the larger scheme of the universe until some proper time.

Now I will confess that I do not think my strength comes purely from my own individuality, I think it arises from a greater reality that is intimately involved with me. I will dispense with metaphysical mumbo-jumbo and call this reality 'God'. Where could my strength for living as I do for so many years come from except from a connection with this reality? Where does the strength of the mountain lion come from if not from this reality? No philosophy that separates me completely from the animal kingdom can command my allegiance. My reasoning powers, which are an aspect of my soul, are an extension of animal instinct; just as my writing this paragraph is an extension of my reasoning powers. No brain science that I am aware of can explain these intuitions. No religion that I am aware of strengthens them. No doubt a reader (should there ever be such) will see these statements as manifestations of an unbridled hubris. He would be right. But I think my hubris stems from a higher reality that I have been privileged to glimpse. This writing has served my purpose in enlightening me about myself and about my position in this utterly absurd world.

~ 33 ~

The other day I went to the general store in town to buy provisions. A young woman I had not seen before was behind the counter. As I was filling my basket, I watched her—graceful figure, good bones, charming expression. A few locks of her blonde hair fell over her forehead, giving an expression of inviting disarray. Then she noticed I was watching her and turned away. I didn't blame her; she must have thought a dirty old man was ogling her. I have to remember how others see me, which is a world apart from how I see myself. I didn't want to make her uncomfortable, I put back the few items I had chosen and left the store.

Ah youth, how I miss you! The primal curse laid on mankind is not work, but growing old. There is no substitute for erotic fulfillment. Whether physical or metaphysical, there is no substitute for it. I remember the poignant ditty:

> All that I own, I mournfully sigh,
> I would give for one night with Miss America Pie.

It is the Faust story, necessarily ending in tragic absurdity. Faust gave away his soul, which I am not prepared to do. But there is no substitute for the feelings of Eros. Youth heedlessly wastes it on orgasmic coupling, giving itself over to blind nature, instead of concentrating on its beauty and uniqueness. It is like gobbling down food at a banquet and feeling ill afterwards. Youth is wasted on the young, as George Bernard Shaw once commented. But there is no substitute for the pleasures of erotic attraction that is a part of youth and, sadly, youth cannot be regained. Human life is inescapably tragic. Those who do not feel this reality have a limited consciousness.

~ 34 ~

Looking over my writings, I find contradictions abounding, which may or may not be a virtue. Emerson wrote that consistency is the hobgoblin of little minds. If that be true, then my mind must be large indeed.

I don't apologize for my contradictions. My soul has many chambers that are constantly being refurbished; they all clamor at different times to announce their contents. Scientific laws must be consistent; a soul has no such requirement. The truth is that I fear to be consistent, since it means my mind has stopped moving onward. The poet-philosopher Fernando Pessoa was once asked during an interview, "What factors have contributed to your development?" His quick response was, "I don't develop, I travel." And so it is truly with me.

~ 35 ~

I need to explain further why I permit myself to become involved with the disreputable idea of God. I don't entertain it because I am suffering and need consolation. I don't believe in Him because I need reassurance about my place in the world. I don't believe because I need a source of strength to face the vicissitudes of living. I certainly don't believe because I want someone to answer my prayers for things I need and for the wellbeing of loved ones. *My feeling for God stems from the hidden wellsprings of my existence.* It arises from the depths of my soul; it is a *mystical feeling.* It is a necessary consequence of awareness of my metaphysical self, which I cannot accept existing as a totally isolated fragment of reality.

All these 'I's and 'My's might put off a reader (should there ever be one) as being insufferable egotism. But this is what my writings are about—I and My and their relationship to reality. *I* am the subject, therefore, I am *subjective*. Reader, *I* and *My* are the same as *You* and *Your*.

Turning to the world of *objective* reality, there seems to be a universal need to acknowledge a reality called God in the English language. It is why religions seem to be invariably present in the annals of civilization. Most of the perceived savants of the twentieth century (e.g., Alfred North Whitehead, Albert Einstein, Martin Heidegger) acknowledged the presence of God in one form of another. Heidegger, for many the guru of existential philosophy (he didn't like the term) who some think to have been a crypto-Catholic, is said to have published a paper at the end of his life titled "Only a god can save us" (Karen Armstrong, *A History of God*). I have not had access to it. But the title reminds me of Voltaire's famous aphorism, "If there were no God, it would be necessary to invent him."

This brings me to William James who might have been stimulated by Voltaire to say if belief in God 'works' for someone, then the belief is true. No apologies are necessary. Since no mortal human being can ever know the truth (John 18:37-38), one might as well invent the truth that works for him says James. Although I have great admiration for William James as a philosopher and writer, his theory of philosophical 'pragmatism' is the ultimate cynicism with respect to the soul and reveals an underlying contempt for it.

Regarding those who since Freud maintain with smug assurance that the idea of God is the consequence of psychological needs and has no scientific basis, I find them to be one-dimensional personalities without spiritual depth. Their dogmas 'work' for them so they have no need for unverifiable metaphysical ideas. The whole trend of modern analytic philosophy supports this attitude. But for me, they represent alien beings that do not share with me the human condition as I have experienced it.

These are the reasons why I permit my mind to entertain the existence of God.

~ 36 ~

Deceit! Deceit! Deceit! Hypocrisy and outright lies! I can't abide these professional politicians using their Christianity to win elections to cushy jobs with fat pensions. Most probably they visit prostitutes and abuse their wives.

People get the political leadership they deserve. One needs the lantern of Diogenes, but I think it would be useless today.

What benefit would I obtain from other people reading what I write? In reality, very little. Most would be bored, uncomprehending, or critical. Some might misunderstand and use my work for purposes of which I would disapprove. I certainly want no admirers. It is only a sense of duty to society that impels me to consider publishing some of my writings. It may well be a bad idea.

In any case, the publishing world is too market oriented to be interested in my writings. There is no place in it for them. I am really best off keeping them within my self-made world where there is an appreciative audience—myself. I have thought out my life and I try to live it to the utmost.

~ 37 ~

It is noteworthy to observe how many initially irreligious thinkers of the nineteenth and early twentieth century toward the latter part of their lives expressed a consciousness of God or some similar concept. In this category fall Heine, Senancour, Amiel, Antero de Quental,

Tolstoy, Berdyaev, Shestov, and others whose names I cannot recall. Even Goethe, the quintessential free spirit, expresses his view at the last page of *Conversations with Eckermann* that God's creative activity was not limited to six days but was ongoing in the guise of human creativity up through Goethe's days.

This tendency seems to have petered out in the twentieth century. Whatever contemporary intellectuals may think privately about ultimate realities, they do not address the issue in their writings. It is 'politically incorrect' to seriously consider God or souls in literary writings. The field is left to religious theologians and fundamentalists who do not represent a truly freethinking intellectual culture and who are not concerned with matters of an intellectual conscience. Famous scientists writing outside their professional realm may quietly admit to a belief in an ultimate reality but that's usually as far as they go. Scholarly treatises on the history of beliefs in God hardly qualify as a metaphysical consciousness. One may wonder if God's purported creative activity manifested through *Homo sapiens* ended in the nineteenth century?

Why is this so? The phenomenon of a late onset spiritual consciousness in an era of science is currently attributed either to an aging-related weakening of the intellectual faculties of an individual or to the vain desire to establish a continuing existence of the self in the face of realization of one's mortality. When one's intellectual rigor is lost through senescence, belief in the existence of God and things as souls move in. Such is the intellectual 'political correctness' of the present age.

However, however...I offer a different explanation. I believe as a person grows older, he also may grow in wisdom (although not predictably) and begins to intuit that there is more to the human condition than the material dimension. The object world of material is no longer so compelling. He becomes aware of his own soul as his real self. He may develop a *metaphysical consciousness*, the highest form of the human condition.

By the twentieth century, however, the cult of scientism had become so firmly established, the object world so pervasive and dominating, that the development of a metaphysical consciousness had become virtually impossible to attain in secular society. This is the contemporary situation. 'Things' have finally become fixed in the societal saddle and they ride mankind in an unchallenged manner. The observation of Emerson has become the reigning rule.

What is to be done? Nothing. Nothing at all. Societies and civilizations must live out their natural courses. An individual can perhaps find a certain exhilaration in functioning creatively within a decaying culture. One can only hope that the poet-philosopher

Robinson Jeffers was wrong in saying that the human race was a failed experiment of God and hope that some new society and new civilization will emerge on the ashes of the old—as historians have often documented. In my humble opinion, the sooner this happens the better.

~ 38 ~

I have given up everything to obtain solitude. I live in the midst of nature, not because it is so propitious for my purposes, but because it frees me from the baneful effects of my society. I don't know anyone personally who has plumbed the depths of solitude to the degree that I have. Even the Christian hermits in the deserts of Syria felt that God incarnated in Jesus Christ was with them. I have no such companion. I am limited to my dog Amigo.

If all I had had was bleak solitude, I think I would have gone mad. Human beings in the course of their development become social creatures and I was no exception. However, I have found something that has replaced the inane and meaningless sociality that was my lot in my early years. This something is the *storehouse of my soul*, described by Antisthenes in the *Banquet* of Xenophon. This storehouse has been filled by my reading, my writing, my thinking. Whenever I feel the lack of social intercourse, I draw upon my storehouse. It provides me with a far higher quality of spiritual nourishment than any sociality available to me. It has never failed me. Periodically, I refill my storehouse with new readings, new writings, and new thoughts.

If I had lived among the type of individuals described in Xenophon's *Banquet*, I might have been satisfied to live socially in the world in which I grew up. But such has not been the case. I have never attended a dinner party remotely resembling *Banquet*. Instead, I have always been surrounded, in or out of banquets, by drugs or alcohol, gluttony or gourmandise, pseudo-intellectual platitudes, and the most banal type of conversation. I even grew to regard my career in philosophy with contempt. I was not successful in the institution of marriage. So I retreated to the forest and stocked the storehouse of my soul.

It is worth reflecting on the Attic society described by Xenophon in *Banquet*. The banquet was a historically known event occurring in 421 B. C. during one of the great Panathenaic games conducted annually in Athens. They might be compared to annual state fairs in the United States, except with more emphasis on athletic competition. The philosophical discourse conducted during the banquet is remarkable in depth and range. There is no reason, however, to think that this particular banquet was unique for the times. Others might have been just as profound.

Banquet gives the lie to any claim for 'progress' of culture or civilization. These Athenians seemed to have done quite well without electrification, motorized transport, or computers. Instead, there seem to be *high points* of civilization, of which Periclean Athens is certainly one of the highest. I will refrain from rating my own, but my way of life speaks for itself to the question.

Finding a valuable book is like finding a pearl in oysters, one has to crack open a great many to find one that is truly enlivening. No doubt that is why Marcus Aurelius says "Away with books!" early in his meditations. But if one had listened to Marcus, he never would have read his Meditations. Paraphrasing John Donne, I think "books mingle souls!" Books that enliven, enlighten, and enrich one's soul exist; they should be sought after and treasured like valuable pearls. It is just that they are hard to find.

~ 39 ~

About God—somewhere, Socrates asks rhetorically how he can ever know the truth about anything when his ideas are always changing. This is the problem I have of my idea of God; my idea of him changes day by day. Today, I will try again to provide some stability to my thoughts about him.

Human beings throughout history seem to have had a psychological need for a concept of God, although the nature of this concept has varied greatly. Since I am a human being, there is no reason why I should not have a similar need—and it is clear to me that I do. The devil is in the details, however, and the details about God are most perplexing for a person seriously searching for truth.

Christians today—unlike the scholastics of medieval times and a few contemporary seminarians—do not worry themselves about God's nature. They believe that He exists and made himself incarnate in Jesus Christ. All that is required is to accept Jesus as one's savior. There is a two-thousand-year tradition behind this point of view so it is easy for those who need God's presence to accept it. For me, however, not being raised in Christianity and having a strong intellectual conscience, it doesn't work. The psychologically naive idea that if you first have faith, then afterwards everything becomes clear, sounds to me like a piece of blatant sophistry. My rational ability is too precious to be sacrificed to such an implausible thought. It is cousin to philosophical pragmatism. Since I have never received any private revelation that Jesus of Nazareth was the Son of God, I can't go that route. Moreover, the history of Christian civilization does not reassure me that Christianity has much to offer mature individuals in terms of spiritual development—as I understand the meaning of 'spirituality'. These remarks apply to a lesser degree to Judaism and to a greater degree to Islam. Both of these two Abrahamic religions require a greater suspension of my intellectual conscience than I am prepared to make.

System-making philosophers generally built into their systems abstruse concepts of God that were difficult for ordinary individuals to comprehend. One of the most recent was Paul Tillich who developed the concept of God as 'The Ultimate Concern' or 'The Metaphysical Ground'. This is in effect no different from Hegel's 'Absolute Spirit' or Heidegger's mystical 'Being'. The God of Spinoza falls into the same category. These are unsatisfactory substitutes for those who need 'God the Father'. The real issue is deciding between Freud's view that God is a substitute father figure, originating in primitive societies, that needs to be discarded in the modern scientific era and the mystical flights of the Jewish Abraham Joshua Heschel who thought a depth religion was needed to recapture the awe, mystery, and wonder of an individual's confrontation with God (*Man Is Not Alone*). The Christian theologian Rudolf Otto had expressed similar thoughts in his influential book *The Idea of the Holy*.

In considering all of the above ideas, I have come to the opinion that the most pertinent approach to obsolete religions is the concept put forth by Ludwig Feuerbach in his landmark work entitled *The Essence of Christianity*.

The book was published in the middle of the nineteenth century and for an inexplicable reason has dropped out of western culture. Perhaps the combined hostility of both Christianity and Marxism has something to do with it. Feuerbach basically asserted that the concept of God was a *projection* of man's own spirit into an external God, thereby alienating himself from his own nature. Karl Marx liked the idea of 'alienation' but applied it to economic servitude rather than religion. As was Marx's habit, he virulently attacked Feuerbach in print. Fundamentalist Christians like Karl Barth have also attacked Feuerbach, because for them the identification of God with man was blasphemy. (In Harper Torchbook's reedition of the book, the editors saw fit to assign the introductory essay to Barth.) Later, Feuerbach developed the notion of an abstract 'humanity', an idea that does not fit into contemporary existential philosophy. But Feuerbach's basic concept expressed in *The Essence of Christianity* deserves much consideration in my judgment.

So I am back where I started from concerning God—uncertainty. But I still feel the issue is a necessary one for every individual who is seriously interested in his own soul to ponder over. Worst of all is to abandon metaphysical thinking for the smug assuredness of a soulless scientism.

What then is the conclusion? Is there no 'ultimate concern' to which one's soul can relate? I think now that I will never know the real meaning of the term God until my demise. Perhaps after that, the mystery will be clarified—although I am not counting on it. Meanwhile, one must soldier on within the human condition.

~ 40 ~

Anticipation of the day of my demise: "OFFICER—I have written what I know and done what I can. Now I deliver my soul to you for judgment."

~ 41 ~

Early one morning, my dog Amigo started barking frantically. There was a knock on my door. I thought it might be a smuggler who was in trouble. But then I saw a Border Patrol vehicle through the window. It irritated me that they should be bothering me so early in the morning. When I opened the door, there was the officer —a woman!

"There was a report that suspicious activity was going on this way," she said in a musical voice. "I wanted to check if you had seen anything—and if you are all right."

In spite of my half-awake state, I couldn't help noticing her striking appearance. She was tall, taller than I was, slim, light-gray eyes and platinum hair. There was no wedding band (something I always look for in women). I guessed she must have been in her mid-thirties. If she had been a man, I would have given a curt answer and sent him on his way. But this situation was different. Suddenly I became quite uncomfortable.

"No," I stammered, "I...I don't think I've seen anything. What did you hear?"

"Our patrol vehicle saw a break in the fence and many footprints not far from here. It looks like a group has crossed over."

We went on this way for a few minutes. I could see she was wondering about me. The Border Patrol knew I lived an isolated life out here and it probably piqued her curiosity. I screwed up my courage and invited her in. My interior was in its usual disheveled state, with books and papers scattered everywhere. I became even more embarrassed because she was obviously taken aback by my living conditions.

"What do you do here?" she asked faintly.

I tried to explain but my explanations sounded incoherent to me. I was like a shy schoolboy trying to talk to a girl. Even through my nervousness, I was annoyed at myself, a mature person with a philosophical mind, incapable of being at ease with a woman. I tried to make the best of it, conducting myself in as dignified a manner as I could. Fortunately, she was amused and was kind to me.

"OK," she finally said. "Sorry to bother you so early. I'd better leave now. I'll report to the office that you haven't seen anything unusual." I restrained myself from foolishly saying I hope I see you again. She got into her vehicle and drove off. I did have an inkling of why I was so nervous and it distressed me.

Whenever I have a visitor, it takes some time before I can recover from the intrusion and resume my life. This time it was worse. I could not get my Border Patrol visitor out of my mind for the rest of the day—I never had learned her name. I was reminded of the absolute prohibitions the Christian hermits of antiquity had against women visitors. It was not the women's problem; it was the hermits' problem. A man who has had no contact with women for long time periods cannot be expected to deal appropriately with erotic surges upon being confronted with an attractive female. It is just beyond human capacities. I can't say I have been subject to temptations like those of St. Anthony, but I can understand them.

Furthermore, age does not immunize one against Eros. In my own case, I have found that decay of genital sexual functions does not inhibit erotic desires. If anything, it intensifies them. Like a blind person who develops heightened auditory and tactile acuity, sexual desire in later life can powerfully manifest itself through alternative routes. The surge of sex is a psychological and metaphysical phenomenon exhibited at all ages. The elderly should feel no sense of shame for erotic feelings or for responding to them. There is no longer concern with unwanted procreation!

So I lectured to myself after the nameless Border Patrol agent had disappeared down the road.

~ 42 ~

I first became aware of the Berliner Max Stirner (1806–1856) during my graduate student days in New York when I was toying with the idea of Anarchism as a viable political philosophy and as a way of life. Among the people I knew, Stirner was looked upon as one of the theoretical originators of Anarchism, but not relevant for modern times. I forgot about him for a long time, but recently I have rediscovered him. He didn't write much; his *opus magnum* and only book is entitled *Der Einzige und Sein Eigentum*, which in English translation has received the absurd title 'The Ego and Its Own.' This is a meaningless expression for readers; worse than translating Nietzsche's *Übermensch* as 'Superman.' My title for Stirner's book would be 'The Unique Individual and His Possessions.' The play on the German words is lost in English.

Without dwelling on the faults of Stirner's book—and there are many—I will say that its principal virtue, a virtue that outweighs all its faults, is that it stands up for the importance and rights of the individual, *Der Einzige*, as the neglected truth of western, especially German, civilization. The book begins with the sarcastic statement (my translation):

> What then is my 'affair' (*die Sache*) supposed to be! Before everything, the 'good' cause, then God's cause, the cause of mankind, truth, freedom, humanity, justice, then the cause of my people, my prince, my country, finally, the cause of spirituality, and a thousand other causes. Only *my* cause should never be my own cause. "Fie upon the egoist who thinks only of himself!" Let's see then, how they manage *their* affairs, those for whose causes we work, devote ourselves, and about whom we are enthusiastic.

Stirner's entire book is dedicated to revealing the error of the unique individual in giving himself over to alien causes. Only for what is *his own*, should he devote himself. His own self ought to be what is important to him, the rest is illusion and error. In the final paragraph of his introduction, Stirner expresses his opinions more directly:

> Away then with every affair that is not absolutely and entirely my affair! You think my cause must be at least a 'good cause'? What is good, what is bad? I am my own cause and I am neither good nor bad. Neither [terms] have any meaning for me.

And then finally, the clinching statement:

> *Mir geht nichts über mich!*—there is nothing more important to me than myself!

One can see how Stirner's book outraged every important group in society, especially the German society of Stirner's era. He was vilified by religious organizations, philosophical academia, patriotic interest groups, social welfare circles, and just about everyone else who had a place In German society. The Communists were particularly hard on him. The two ideologues of communism, Marx and Engels, launched a typically vicious *ad hominem* attack on Stirner in the essay *The German Ideology*. One can suspect that a book that unleashed so much hostility must have a painful truth present in it.

The painful truth, as I see it, is that individuals do not value their own unique selves as much as they should, and they give themselves over to any cause that relieves them of the burden of self-valuation. What is necessary is not superficial selfishness, but self-respect in its deepest meaning, respect for one's own soul. It is in this area that Stirner fails, since he was the product of the newly developing, materialist worldview of his times and he rejected metaphysical consciousness. For him, as for most freethinkers of that era (and ours), the soul is just another illusion propagated by religious tyrants who want to dominate human beings.

The literary defects of *Der Einzige und Sein Eigentum* are evident from its first pages. The book cries for careful editing. It is amazing to me that he was able to find a reputable editor in Leipzig, and even more amazing that the book enjoyed a brief period of popularity among German intellectuals of that era. Then Stirner's star faded and now he is rarely mentioned in textbooks of philosophy. This is regrettable because Stirner does have an important point of view deserving of consideration.

Stirner, like most German philosophers, is verbose and repetitive. He is very often sarcastic, and sometimes it is difficult to tell where sarcasm ends and his own views begin. Occasionally he mentions self-development, but does not 'develop' this idea. More often, he says *Der Einzige* is perfect, although he probably would have admitted this to be hyperbole. But the faults of the book must be forgiven, because of the significance of its central message.

Max Stirner does a great service in emphasizing the existential significance of the individual. However, what does he offer him? Power, Ownership, and Self-Enjoyment.

The last of these is the solution of Goethe's poem *Vanitas, Vanitorum, Vanitas!*, whose first line is the title of Stirner's introduction to his book ("I have staked my affair on Nothing."). Feasting, singing, and drinking is the answer to life for Goethe's 'I' in the poem. (Goethe's own opinion is characteristically elusive.) Boccacio said the same in *The Decameron* (also concealing his own view), as did the unknown author of the biblical *Ecclesiastes*, who clearly disapproved of asceticism. Stirner extols the primary virtue of "using yourself up" (*Verwerte dich!*) in the pursuit of happiness. Regarding the motive for his writing, Stirner compares it to the chirping of birds in trees.

As far as power, ownership, and self-enjoyment are concerned—goals that Stirner advocates, I know where these have gotten people with whom I am familiar. If this be freethinkers' earthly heaven, I think I prefer some other place.

~ 43 ~

Summer is 'mini-monsoon' season in southeastern Arizona. The other evening, a particularly severe one roared through my section of the forest. The thunder was deafening; the winds were later said to be up to 60 mph; rain and hail the size of golf balls accompanied the wind.

My defective roof leaked in a dozen places and the windows rattled to the beat of an imaginary rock band. Poor Amigo was frightened out of his wits, refusing to leave my side. I could dimly see the dirt road next to my house had become a sea of mud and broken branches. Then to top it all, the electricity gave out. I was left in the gloom of the storm.

I have to admit that I felt much as Amigo did, terrified, except there was no one to turn to for reassurance. My benevolent solitude had turned into a fearsome isolation. Suddenly it became apparent that even in my remote location, how dependent I was on society. Without electrification, without motorized transport, without any means of communication to the outside world, I was totally at the mercy of an enraged nature. I felt my survival was in question. Pervasive fear had taken the place of my usual Stoical calm.

I did survive the storm. The monsoon ended during the night. The next day the sun was shining and the world looked different. My electricity had thankfully come back on. The road dried quickly in the bright sunlight and I was able to clear away the branches from my vehicle. The forest was as before: peaceful, beautiful, a place of refuge. Even Amigo was willing to go outside to take care of his needs.

But the memory remains. I wondered how the Apaches had dealt with the extremities of nature. Did they have the degree of fear that had gripped me? The white pioneers of not so long ago in this land were without the supports of technology or societal organizations. How did they manage? The records they left behind don't say anything to my knowledge about mini-monsoons. Their flimsy structures might not have survived. Some of them even lived in tents. I am left with the inescapable conclusion that my society with its technology has made me utterly dependent upon it in times of stress, physically and psychologically. Even more to the point for me, how did all the great literature of the world get produced without computers, word processors, even typewriters? Has the word-processing technology upon which I depend resulted in greater literature, especially in philosophy, than was the case in the past? The answer is evident; in fact, I believe there is an inverse relationship between use of technology and 'great' literature of any type. How sobering it is for me to realize I am dependent upon an all-encompassing soulless technology. The DNA of scientism has entered in my bones.

~ 44 ~

I am going to copy a page from *The Private Papers of Henry Ryecroft* (1903) by George Gissing (one my favorite writers), because it expresses more clearly than I can my feeling about scientism. I have made a few minor alterations in the quote:

> The progress of the human species has been founded on one thing and one thing alone—the development of consciousness. Religious or scientific habits that stand in the way of full recognition of this truth impede human development. The great scientific pioneers of the past have enlarged our consciousness of the milieu in which life exists and develops—Copernicus, Newton, Darwin, Einstein, Sherrington, to name a few. They have always avoided the hubris of imagining their theories could be extended to include that which created them. However, some twentieth century scientifically-minded intellectuals, beginning with Sigmund Freud, have been more arrogant and have extended their reach to everything in sight—including the human mind. But the lesson of human culture, of which science is a subset, does not support this endeavor. Science has no intellectual basis at the present time for reductionist explanations of consciousness; it has working for it only the prestige deriving from its technology. This prestige, and the influence associated with it, has been frightening for a long time to those with the vision to see beyond technology.

The Victorian era writer George Gissing then penned the following prior to two World Wars when there was less disaffection with modern technology than there is at present—attesting to the profundity of Gissing's insights:

> I wonder whether there are many men who have the same feeling with regard to 'science' as I have? It is something more than a prejudice; often it takes the form of a dread, almost a terror. Even those branches of science which are concerned with things that interest me—which deal with plants and animals and the heaven of stars—even these I cannot contemplate without uneasiness, a spiritual disaffection; new discoveries, new theories, however they engage my intelligence, soon weary me and in some way depress. When it comes to the other kinds of science—the sciences blatant and ubiquitous—the science by which men become millionaires—I am possessed by an angry hostility, a resentful apprehension. This was born in me, no doubt; I cannot trace it to circumstances of my life, or to any particular moment of my mental growth. My boyish delight in Carlyle [Thomas] doubtless nourished the temper, but did not Carlyle so delight me because of what was already in my mind? I remember as a lad, looking at machinery with a shrinking uneasiness, which, of course, I did not understand; I remember the sort of disturbed contemptuousness with which, in times of 'examinations,' I dismissed 'science papers.' It is intelligible enough to me now, that unformed fear: the ground of my antipathy has grown clear enough. I hate and fear 'science' because of my conviction that, for a long time to come if not forever, it will be the remorseless enemy of mankind. I

see it destroying all simplicity and gentleness of life, all the beauty of the world; I see it restoring barbarism under a mask of civilization; I see it darkening men's minds and hardening their hearts: I see it bringing a time of vast conflicts, which will pale into insignificance 'the thousand wars of old [Tennyson], and likely as not, will whelm all the laborious advances of mankind in blood-drenched chaos.

Hyperbole? Perhaps, but justifiable hyperbole. Today, one may question whether Ryecroft (a.k.a. George Gissing) was born with an antiscientific bent of mind; rather we may think that it was the consequence of his growing up in a rapidly industrializing England, to which were added his own extraordinary perceptions.

~ 45 ~

I see more and more *illegales* coming through the forest toward destinations in the states. The Border Patrol does not seem to be able to control the flow. Whether this is good or bad for America, I cannot say, but *El destino se manifieste*, as I once read in a Mexican newspaper regarding this northward emigration. Manifest Destiny is not limited to the United States. There is no fighting destiny—as the Apaches of southern Arizona learned to their chagrin. What was formerly Mexico might yet become Mexican again, demographically if not politically.

~ 46 ~

Anyone who might become acquainted with my life and read my writings might think I am extremely pessimistic, a misanthrope—a hater of mankind—and one without any beliefs or values. Well, I do admit to a strong misanthropic streak and a deep-seated contempt for the values of my society. But that is not all that there is of me. *I believe in my own soul*; I believe in its importance, its goodness, even its destiny. I have a *reverence* for my soul. I work hard to develop it further. In this regard, I feel myself to be akin to Walt Whitman who wrote *Song of Myself*, a poem that set the stage for much of the subsequent development of American poetry. Like Whitman, I am an optimist when it comes to my own soul.

Naturally, aficionados of American poetry might laugh derisively to hear me comparing myself to Whitman. Whitman was a poet, which I am not, and a master of the English language. Whitman was a democrat and loved the idea of *humanity*, neither of which feelings I have. He was a materialist and a pantheist; none of these labels apply to me. Whitman believed in America, I clearly do not. Whitman became famous, I have not; and fate willing, I will live out my life in my private condition. But Whitman believed in his own soul and in this I share his feeling. I might have prefaced whatever I have written with the immortal lines that begin *Song of Myself*, "I celebrate myself and sing myself." He celebrated his body and his soul, but as he became old and infirm, he dropped the former. I celebrate my soul, more now than when I was Walt's thirty-seven years of age. I feel justified in comparing myself with him since we both think ourselves to be a "kosmos, of Manhattan the son." He is my 'camerado' and we both believe that "nothing, not God, is greater to one than one's self is."

I am a rank optimist when it comes to my soul and that is what counts. Those who love humanity, but not their own souls, are destined for a disappointing end of their existence. I do not think there will be a disappointing end to my existence, even if I don't know now what that end will be. I have worked to develop my soul and I expect to be rewarded for my efforts. What could be more optimistic than this belief!

~ 47 ~

I have been living in my forest retreat for more years than I care to remember. I wonder if it is time to think about leaving. Perhaps it is time for me to have new experiences and a new life. The original reasons for my coming here may not be as valid as they were before. Should I try again to live among people and obtain the experiences of living in contact with others? Thoreau lived less than two years at Walden Pond; when he left there, he offered the reason that he had other lives to lead. I am not too old to lead a different life.

But where to go? Thoreau had his parents' house to retreat to and Concord to live in. I have no such resources. I have no living family, as far as I know. My former college or post office connections no longer exist for me. My occasional sorties into Tucson have taught me I cannot live in that city, or for that matter, in any big city. Small town life would be hardly any better for me than living in the forest—and without the anonymity that I prize. The Concord I have always idealized disappeared many generations ago. Today it is just a nest of museums surrounded by a suburbia that would have revolted Thoreau.

Mexico? Expatriate life with its aimlessness and alcoholism? I could afford to live in Mexico but life there does not appeal to me. Besides, I have never been able to speak Spanish very well. Expat life elsewhere is too complex for me to attempt; in any case, my slender income would probably not allow me to live in Europe, which is the only possibility I could consider.

The unfortunate truth is that there is no place for me in any society. I am like a man without a country. Perhaps I should take matters into my own hands and call it *finis*. I have lived my allotted three score and ten years and am approaching four score. My eyesight is weakening and I don't hear very well. Maybe it is time to leave the banquet table, as some ancient Roman said. But how to leave? I think it was Dorothy Parker who, after considering all the uncertain and unpleasant methods of suicide, decided it was easier just to live. It might come to that with me. I will have to carry on in the one place where I have truly flourished.

O my soul, I will not desert thee!

The ancient Greek philosopher Heraclitus, who must have had an isolation-loving personality similar to mine, was afflicted with 'dropsy' (generalized swelling of body tissues) according to Diogenes Laertius. He left his solitude to seek medical care. Apparently, the doctors could not help him and he died under unpleasant circumstances—again according to D. L. I don't think I would ever leave my cabin to seek medical care. No need at my age to interfere with the workings of the goddesses of fate.

~ 48 ~

The Greek Cynic movement of antiquity has always attracted me. There is something about the personality of its founders—Antisthenes, Diogenes, Crates—that fascinates me. Cynicism as a philosophical movement and as a way of life lasted, with ups and downs, for almost a thousand years during antiquity, indicating there must have been something meaningful to it for the people of that period. It disappeared, along with most of the rest of antique culture other than the Christian one, when barbarians overran Europe and Christian monks became the custodians of literature.

Diogenes of Sinope, the founder of the Cynic way of life and thought, has no credibility among the scholars and historians of contemporary philosophy. He is seen as a comical figure, a noisy clever hobo, who contributed nothing to culture. That is because he was the great naysayer of Athens—someone who rejected every aspect of Greek tradition and culture, especially the increasing complexity of its philosophy. Philosophy textbooks of today do not mention his name, except on occasion to mention the absurd side of Greek thought. I don't need to further describe the movement, which can be found in histories of ancient Greece and particularly in a book that I treasure, *Les Cyniques Grec* by Leoncé Paquet. The preface of

Paquet's book contains a most insightful description of the Cynic movement.

The Greek Cynics put the wellbeing of their individual selves ahead of all else in their scale of values. They refused to degrade themselves by acceding to customs of a society they saw to be hypocritical, pleasure-oriented, corrupt, and ignorant of the true needs of human beings. They thought the institutions of their day did not answer any of these needs and made matters worse by introducing unnecessary restrictions into the lives of people. The elaborate explications of philosophers like Plato and Aristotle they thought worthless, only distracting gullible followers from their own circumstances. Most important of all, the Cynics *lived out* their beliefs, believing that activity of the mind separated from its bodily correlates was useless.

I maintain the Cynic way of life was 'spiritual' because it reflected values of the soul—asceticism, simplicity of living, frankness of speech, return to nature (as they understood nature), flight from harmful constraints, skepticism of established customs, and, above all, freedom of thought. They believed in philosophy as love of wisdom. They tried to define wisdom according to their lights. They committed themselves as spiritual beings to the Greek concept of *arête* (αρετη)—not happily translated into English as 'virtue', given the usual association of the word with morality. 'Excellence' is a better translation; for the Greek Cynics, arête meant excellence of character. They refused to act in any way that would compromise their aspiration for arête of character. Henry David Thoreau has been called the American Cynic—the truth of which anyone who is familiar with his life will recognize. (No one would refer to Thoreau as 'virtuous.') One could justly say that Thoreau was a long delayed last gasp of Greek Cynicism; there have been no more after him to fit the pattern.

It is apparent that the contemporary meaning of the English word 'cynical' is not applicable to the Greek Cynics. They may have been cynical about society, but for the most part, they were anything but cynical about their own ideals and way of life. Greek Cynicism had a varied history over its long existence, not always with admirable representatives after its first efflorescence in Athens. The total rejection of societal customs led to caricatures of its nature by conventional citizens. Its founder Diogenes excelled in sarcasm, invective, and the art of shocking his contemporaries. But he was sincere in his beliefs; most societies with their habit of misusing individuals need a healthy dose of the nay saying that is an important feature of Greek Cynicism. Most important of all, however, is the necessity of recognizing the *spiritual* nature of the Cynic movement, as evidenced by their reverential commitment to honest spiritual values in their own lives.

~ 49 ~

Periodically, the question arises within me: why do I continually write out my thoughts? Why do I expend so much effort on putting them down on paper when I know there will be no readers for them? Sooner or later, I always arrive at the same answer; I write to develop my soul. Writing is to my soul as exercise is to my body; it enlarges, deepens, and gives new substance to it. But then I go further and ask myself: to what purpose does all this spiritual development serve? Is there any purpose to it?—or am I only engaging in a kind of mental narcissism?

But if I look outside of myself, I can pose the same question to everything I see or hear. What purpose all forms of life? What purpose propagation? Even further, what purpose the universe and all within it? Asking these questions makes it clear to me that any purpose in the ultimate scheme of things is beyond my ken as a mere human being. However, when I penetrate into my mind, I find that I possess an unshakable faith that there is a purpose for developing my soul. It is only that I am not meant to know this purpose, just as Moses was not meant to 'know' the promised land of the Israelites.

~ 50 ~

The term *graviton* has just come to my attention. It is said to be a hypothetical sub-particle that explains the force of gravitation. However, on looking into the matter, I find that astrophysicists are now saying that gravitation is not due to a force at all, but to a 'perturbation' in the space-time continuum. This latter idea is derived from Einstein's theory of general relativity. I am using these terms freely but I really don't understand what they mean. Too bad there is not a modern-day Molière to write a comedy about all these esoteric theories.

The worldviews of physics today require expression by mathematical formulas, not images or concepts. They are in an alien language that I cannot assimilate into my mind—nor do I want to. I have already heard that my soul is just a wiring mesh of fibers in my brain, or worse yet, a vast system of software like the entrails of a computer. These thoughts evoke a harsh hostility in me, similar to that expressed by Henry Ryecroft in the book of George Gissing. I refuse to be characterized by wiring diagrams or microchips. 'I' am something more than the soulless maze of neurons in my cranium. Anyone who attempts to tell me otherwise is my sworn enemy with whom I will have nothing to do, if I can help it. Science, as Henry Ryecroft wrote, is like a barbarian army threatening to invade and destroy my land, my home, my way of being. Perhaps it will succeed, but I will fight it to the bitter end.

The long forgotten (by me) Psalm 24 unexpectedly comes to my mind, which I look up for its details: "The earth is the Lord's and the fullness thereof, the world, and they that dwell therein." I know I would rather the world and its fullness belong to the Lord than to science. My soul assuredly does not pant after science. Without some sense of holiness in the world, the effort of living human life is not worth the trouble. Many have thought the same. "Be holy," it says in Leviticus (19:2), and so say I as well.

It has been observed that the Devil can quote Scripture for his own ends. Perhaps, but there is often much wisdom in what the Devil says. Goethe reveals Mephistopheles to be far wiser than Herr Doktor Faust. The seeker of wisdom knows how to quote either Scripture or the Devil for his own ends. Therefore, I repeat the scriptural admonition "Be holy" because it is the only route I know toward my own salvation.

Of course, it is natural to want elaboration on what is meant by the term 'holy.' I know of no better source than the book previously quoted by Rudolf Otto entitled *The Idea of the Holy*, especially the chapter 'The Holy as an *a priori* category,' Part I. The title of this chapter states the basic concept of the book. The potential for the sense of holiness is ingrained in the human soul. (Part II can be dispensed with as the Christian cleric in Otto took over.) One need not be a Christian, however, to gain much from Otto's book. As an interesting aside, he admits that the English version is superior to the German original.

~ 51 ~

I have decided to recount to myself the details of my daily life—in this way, I should be able to get a handle of how I live and whether any changes are in order. I arise early, often before 6 AM. The first thing I do is to make a large cup of strong coffee in order to fully rouse myself from the embrace of Morpheus. By then, Amigo is jumping up and down at the door, barking furiously. I know what he wants; he is anxious for his morning walk but he has to wait until I finish my coffee. Then we set out. We have a choice of various directions so that the walk is not repetitive. We walk a long time, often up to two hours. Amigo likes to choose his own path, although I know he will eventually rejoin me.

Most seasons, the forest is wonderful in the early mornings, as long as I don't wait too long to start out. Everything is fresh and clear, and the birds are out in force. Nature is still king here, since the vileness of human development has not yet taken over. I have been walking these paths for many years now, yet there is always something new to be seen and sometimes I have to work hard to find my way home. This is the time when I most appreciate my way of life here and it is often when I do my best thinking.

At home usually by mid-morning, Amigo and I finally take breakfast. For me, this always consists of a bowel of dry cereal and raisins covered with regular milk—not the watery skimmed variety. Sometimes, depending on my appetite, I also have a toasted English muffin, of which I keep a large supply in my little freezer. More coffee, as well, which I sip throughout the morning. Then, while Amigo sleeps, I settle down to write at my ancient Smith Corona word processor. Since I do not write for publication, I have no definite scheme to follow. I write about whatever seems important to me at the time—like this review of my usual day. Rarely do my writings consist of more than a thousand words. But since I write daily, they do pile up. I learn a great deal from these private writings of mine, both at the time of their composition and afterwards, when I reread them, anytime from a few weeks to a few years later. The ones that don't seem worthwhile, I discard.

I write for one to two hours, depending on my energies and my investment in the topic. None of this all day writing for me that consumes the brains of professional writers and scholars. I stop writing when I feel

I have said my piece. Sometime in the early afternoon, I have my main meal of the day, *la comida*, as they say across the border. Rice and beans are my main staples, since I can store them easily. The beans come from a can since I don't have the patience to prepare my own. But there are many interesting varieties of canned beans: Cuban, black, garbanzo, pinto, and more. They add variety to my meal. The rice is always steamed white Jasmine. Sometimes, I have hard-boiled eggs, if I feel ambitious. Raw carrots are my vegetable. I never have meat at home, not for any principle, but because I like to keep things simple.

I know my diet is deficient in fruits and vegetables; these are difficult for me to obtain on any sort of regular basis. Occasionally I buy apples at the local market, but they are expensive and usually not good. Once in a very great while, I will dine at a nearby steak house and treat myself to a real steak. I must admit I do like a fine medium-rare New York steak, but it is hard on my budget so I can't do it too often. As far as drinks are concerned, cold water is always the order of the day. I have never acquired a taste for beer, and wine puts me to sleep. It is very annoying to find myself falling asleep when I want to read or write.

Sometime after *comida,* I turn to my library. Usually I read old favorites that I haven't read in a long time or that are connected to my writing. I never read any contemporary novels or non-fiction, since I have found they do not hold my interest. If there could be exceptions, I don't have the time or inclination to seek them out. I'm afraid I don't contribute much to the publishing industry. As far as what I do read, this has to be a subject for a different writing.

Now I seem to be more interested in writing than reading. More and more, I find myself returning to writing in the afternoons. I remember Schopenhauer's dictum, "Reading is thinking with another person's brain." This dictum may finally be sinking into my own brain. But I can't deny that my mind has been greatly expanded by reading, and I don't know how I could live without my library. Once in a while, I become aware of some book I would like to own. Then I take my obsolescent computer to the local library that has Wi-Fi and hope that the computer works. If it does, I will order what I want from Amazon. Amazon has been a great boon to me in my isolated life far from any bookstores.

Supper for me is light, usually cheese and crackers. A luxury I permit myself afterwards is an ounce or so of brandy. I do enjoy good brandy, but not too close to bedtime as it can interfere with my night's sleep. But if it does, I feel the pleasure of a snifter of brandy is worth getting up in the middle of the night. Evenings, Amigo and

I go for a shorter walk. By 9 PM, however, I am usually in bed for the night.

There it is—how I spend my days and nights. I am never bored; I spend my leisure hours thinking, reading, or writing. Always I am able to draw from the 'storehouse of my mind,' to use a phrase I quote often from Antisthenes, one of my favorite Greek philosophers. I am free at all times to be myself, I don't have to don any masks, I have plenty of leisure to do what I want or to only think as the occasion warrants. I never have to generate meaningless chatter. There is no better place to live my life than where I am at this time. I have more to say about what I read, but it will have to wait for another writing session.

~ 52 ~

The sayings of Jesus have played an important part in my life. I have six different Bibles but I mainly read the Gospels, to which I often turn. One of them is a New Testament with interlinear Greek and English. I like to compare translations since I am aware of the uncertainties involved in reading Jesus at third hand (Aramaic>Greek>English). The parts of the Gospels that have to do with his activities, his miracles, and the circumstances of his death, I ignore. I don't know what to believe or not to believe about them. The events after the crucifixion, I absolutely ignore as pure legends. But his sayings reveal his mind to me; I don't think any of his disciples were capable of fabricating his sayings. I am going to write down the ones that have been most significant for me, reminding myself that their context is important in really appreciating them. Most are from Matthew, because that is the gospel I have read the most. They are all taken from the King James translation, which is my favorite. My one-liners below them ought not to take away the focus from Jesus' sayings themselves:

Mt 4:4   "Man shall not live by bread alone."
The essential statement about spiritual life.

Mt 5:15   "Neither do men light a candle, and put it under a bushel, but on a candlestick; and it giveth light unto all that are in the house."
The justification for disseminating one's writings—which I plead guilty of not following. Jesus didn't know my situation.

Mt 5:48   "Ye cannot serve God and Mammon."
How true! But hard to consistently follow.

Mt 7:6   "Give not which is holy unto the dogs, neither cast your pearls before swine, lest they trample them under their feet, and turn again and rend you."

The case against my publishing.

Mt 10:17 "But beware of men: for they will deliver you up to the councils, and they will scourge you in their synagogues."

My experience exactly.

Mt 10:36 "And a man's foes shall be they of his own household."

A universal truth for exceptional individuals.

Mt 12:34 "O generation of vipers, how can ye, being evil, think good things?"

Was Jesus thinking of book critics?

Mt 15:11 "Not that which goeth into the mouth defileth a man but that which cometh out of the mouth, this defileth a man."

The reason to stay away from cocktail parties.

Mt 16:26 "For what is a man profited, if he shall gain the whole world and lose his own soul?"

Eternal wisdom; but, if one doesn't believe in the soul's existence, the saying is meaningless.

Mt 19:24 "And again I say unto you, it is easier for a camel [or thick rope] to go through the eye of a needle, than for a rich man to enter into the kingdom of heaven."

Self-evident.

Mt 22:37 " Thou shalt love the Lord thy God with all thy heart, and with all thy soul, and with all thy mind."

A reminder to me that there may be more to existence than my own soul.

Mt 23:27 "Woe unto you scribes and Pharisees, hypocrites! For ye are like whited sepulchers, which indeed appear beautiful outward, but are full of dead men's bones, and of all uncleanness."

That was my former world.

Mk 2:27 "And he said to them, the Sabbath was made for man, and not man for the Sabbath."

This could be equally said of the Torah, the rest of the Holy Bible, and all religious establishments.

Mk 10:18 "And Jesus said to him, Why callest thou me good? There is none good but one, that is, God."

This seems to me quite persuasive that Jesus did not consider himself a divine, only begotten son.

Mk 12:30 "And thou shall love the Lord thy God with all thy heart, and with all thy soul, and with all thy mind, and with all thy strength."

Repeat of Mt. 22:37, only stronger.

Lk 11:52 "Woe unto you, lawyers! for ye have taken away the key of knowledge: ye entered not in yourselves, and them that were entering in ye hindered."

In my view, applicable to the mainstream monotheistic religions.

Lk 17:21 "...for Behold, the kingdom of God is *within* you."

A key statement by Jesus. See discussion below about the significance of *within*.

Lk 20:25 "And he said unto them, Render therefore unto Caesar the things which be Caesar's, and unto God the things which be God's."

The justification not only for paying taxes, but also for participating in a social contract.

Jn 3:3 "Verily, verily, I say unto thee. Except a man be born again, he cannot see the kingdom of God."

Referable to Lk 17:21.

Jn 4:24 "God is a spirit." (πνευμα ο θεοσ)

An essential concept but I doubt that Jesus said it.

Jn 12:43 "For they loved the praise of men more than the praise of God."

A universal failing. One from which I have struggled to become free.

Jn 14:6 "Jesus saith unto him [Thomas], I am the way, the truth, and the life; no man cometh unto the Father, but by me."!!!

I am sure Jesus never said this. It cannot be reconciled with Mk 10:18, which I believe a more reliable expression of Jesus' mind. It is probably a gloss like much else in John.

Jn 18:38   "Pilate saith unto him [Jesus], what is truth?"

Nietzsche said this is the only intelligent statement in the entire New Testament.

Jn 16:33   "In the world ye shall have tribulation, but be of good cheer, I have overcome the world."

Standard Greek Stoic doctrine, but worthy of constant repetition.

Lk 17:20-21   "And when he was demanded of the Pharisees, when the kingdom of God should come, he answered them and said, The kingdom of God cometh not with observation: Neither shall they say, Lo here! or, lo there! for, behold, the kingdom of God is *within* (*entos*, εντοσ) you."

This is a critical statement. Jesus is saying salvation is *within* the individual. But four of my six Bibles translate 'entos' as 'among' or 'in your midst,' implying Jesus himself is the Kingdom of God. Only the King James and the New International Version translate it correctly as *within*. (The latter gives 'among' as an alternative—not true!) This is not just philological hair-splitting; it is a fundamental difference of concept about the nature of the 'Kingdom of God' for individuals. My Greek dictionaries are very clear, 'entos' means 'within' or 'inside' (Liddell & Scott, *Greek-English Lexicon*; *Analytical Greek Lexicon of the Greek New Testament*; *The Classic Greek Dictionary*). Translation of 'entos' as 'among' gives an entirely different meaning to Jesus' statement. 'Entos' (inside) is the opposite of 'ektos' (outside) and they are used in this way in Mt 23:26.

Unless there are variants from the word *entos* in other Greek manuscripts of which I am unaware, there has been an attempt by certain translators to obscure Jesus' saying in order to maintain the dogma that salvation is only possible through Jesus Christ. This is a central Christian dogma that Jesus himself seems not to support as reported in the original Greek of Luke. If the Kingdom of God is *within* one, he has only to become conscious of its presence himself. The idea verges on the concept of the 'wise' man in Greek Stoicism, albeit in a more metaphysical context. One can debate the issue, but there is no excuse for altering Gospel language in translation.

~ 53 ~

Some have said to me that my way of life lacks human contact, warmth, stimulation, support. I admit to all this. All these things were overly important to me until I achieved manhood—but not since. Now they are of less significance and, at times, destructive to my personality. Now solitude is more valuable for me than human interactions. One can make of this admission whatever one wishes.

I rarely have visitors and I never have other than superficial conversations with anyone during my weekly outings for provisions. One person I do talk with occasionally is Richard Schain, the independent philosopher who lives some miles away from me. (I avoid academics like the plague.) I have read some of his books and have found them similar in many ways to my own writings. We have the same worldviews, but his life is very different from mine. He seems to be financially quite well off. Naturally, this must affect our basic feelings about the world. Schain has a charming wife, a large luxurious home, and two expensive vehicles. He lives a completely bourgeois existence compared to my Thoreauvian one. Can a truly independent philosopher arise out of such circumstances? I doubt it. In my view, they limit the range and depth of his writings. Given his situation and style of life, it is to be expected that he desires to market his writings and achieve fame, something I have studiously avoided since my departure from academic life. I write for myself, while Schain writes for a public (which, in fact, seems so far not to have paid much attention to him).

I see nothing of value for myself in publication. What benefit would I derive by others recognizing my name, imitating my thoughts, quoting my carefully thought out sentences, expressing unwanted critiques. No benefit at all, only irritation, aggravation, and loss of privacy. I do not recognize the right of others to even praise my work. The rank commercialism of the literary industries is repulsive to me. I have not written for publication since my unhappy days as a university faculty member. My writings are random, arbitrary, and rarely more than a page or two in length. Sometimes they are only a paragraph. So they are repetitive, so they are contradictory, so they are not 'scholarly'—so much the better. They are an expression of my interior self, and in no way oriented to the outer world. They create my soul, not my reputation.

After reviewing my way of living long and in depth, I have concluded that it is the best one for me at my stage of life. Whether it is best for anyone else, I cannot say. But I believe my soul has flourished in this solitary existence. My life here has been the making of me as a representative of the species *Homo sapiens*. Should I ever leave it, it would not change this reality.

~ 54 ~

My favored books, the books I really treasure, are old friends with whom I meet up every few years, as the occasion warrants. When I open one of these treasured volumes, it is like a reunion with someone I have known well in the past; our paths diverged, and now we have come together again. The books of Nicholas Berdyaev are some of the most treasured of these friends with whom I meet at least every year. I remember when I first came across Berdyaev some thirty years ago in his signature writing *The Meaning of the Creative Act,* superbly translated from the Russian by Donald Lowrie. The first two sentences of his Introduction fell upon me like a ton of bricks: "The human spirit is in prison. Prison is what I call this world, the given world of necessity." This is how I felt at the time; my spirit was in prison. It was exhilarating to find someone who felt the same way and even extend it to a universal abstraction, "the human spirit." Every time I reread it, it has an impact upon me because I believe it was, and still is to a degree, the truth of my condition. I have read much in Berdyaev since then, but nothing has had the impact upon me of that first encounter.

I have a similar feeling when I read the pregnant saying of Friedrich Nietzsche, "The noble soul has reverence for itself" (*Beyond Good and Evil*). I am too prone to overvalue what is outside of myself and to undervalue what is inside myself. Even though they had very different visions of the human condition, I join Nietzsche with Berdyaev because they both acted to stimulate, strengthen, and expand my consciousness, effects that cannot be measured by any scientific means. Very different has been the effect of Fernando Pessoa upon me (*Livro do Desassossego—Book of Discontent*). His semi-autobiographical character Bernardo Soares projects a warmth and an intellectual intimacy that I find intensely satisfying. After spending time with Soares-Pessoa, I feel myself to be part of the human race, something I have doubted in the past. It is interesting to me that Pessoa was thought by those who knew him to be a remote, impenetrable personality. But he created a literary 'alter ego' that is exactly the opposite of what Pessoa was in the flesh.

One book I love to return to is *The Private Papers of Henry Ryecroft* by George Gissing, which I have previously quoted. There is a humanism and nostalgia of Gissing's character that has a beneficial effect upon me. There is none of the forceful intensity of a Berdyaev or of a Nietzsche; instead, one feels a calm acceptance of the limitations of the human condition. Also, there is something about Gissing's evocation of the best aspects of Victorian England that I find most appealing. He has an unmatched capacity to handle the English language. I have previously quoted his distrust and disdain of 'science,' an attitude that I share completely.

I need to mention my high esteem for Marcus Aurelius as a writer and philosopher; it is part of my general esteem of the outstanding features of culture during Greco-Roman antiquity. At its best, antiquity fostered a high regard for the individual and a sense of his capacity for self-development. This was lost upon collapse of the Roman Empire, with the subsequent Christianization of culture that depended upon a 'savior,' rather than on the 'ruling principle' (το ηγεμονικον) of the individual. Marcus in his *Meditations* (the name later applied to his private writings) epitomizes the regard for self in antique culture. Every time I reread him, I gain renewed confidence in my own way of life.

There are many other book friends that I have; perhaps not at the same level of intimacy of those mentioned above. Whenever I become concerned that I have no friends, I realize that it is not true; it is only that my friends are not of this world. Yet they are better friends to me than any I have managed to make in the usual meaning of the term.

~ 55 ~

Concrete accomplishments are at the basis of all American values. 'Get things done,' 'build a life,' 'create wealth,' 'help others'; these and many more are the watchwords by which an individual is supposed to live. If you don't accomplish things, then you are not worth much. A person's life resumé is supposed to contain his accomplishments, ranging from obtaining credentials to productive work.

The significant thing, however, about a human being's life, is not his concrete accomplishments but his non-concrete ones—namely, building his or her own soul. One does not do this by the watchwords mentioned above but by contemplation and meditation on one's life experiences—to which I would add the *expression* of his mental activity in creative form. Every living individual has experiences necessary for contemplative thought—some more than others. The choices of experiences from which the soul can be built are some of the most important decisions of one's life. But the main thing is to believe that building a soul is the single most significant feature of human life and worthy of devotion of one's time and energy. In this era of absence of belief in the soul, such an attitude is difficult to maintain. Regardless of what Jesus warned against, there is no point in worrying about losing one's soul, if one has never been created in the first place.

A person who takes his own soul seriously is often labeled as a *mystic*. This is usually meant in a pejorative sense, implying that the person does not accomplish things, that he is a dreamer and not good for much. All types of mysticisms were prevalent at the time of Jesus of Nazareth, but Christianity (i.e., worship of Jesus) won out, due in no small measure to the administrative abilities of the early Christian bishops. They so impressed the Roman Emperor Constantine that he ceased persecuting the Christians and gave official status to Christianity within the Roman Empire. Many thoughtful individuals, Christian and non-Christian alike, have seen this event as a fateful event. It led to the secular power of the Papacy and the development of autocratic attitudes in Christianity. Later, came the execution of apostates and heretics. Dogma and spirituality are irreconcilable qualities.

The dominance of organized religion over spiritual life in the western world has meant that naysayers have been more important than yeasayers when it is a question of spiritual truthfulness. For all intensive purposes, *sub rosa* atheism and scientism have become dominant. Along with belief in God, belief in the soul has been relegated to back shelf status. Lip service may be paid to traditional religions, but vital belief has disappeared. People believe in their bank accounts, their insurance policies, their salaries or pensions, their houses, their automobiles; but belief in religious ideas is largely a dead letter. I feel it is possible to trace the decline of Christianity to its establishment as the state religion of the Roman Empire. For those who think this to be a farfetched idea, I recommend reading *The Age of Constantine the Great* by the eminent nineteenth century Swiss historian Jacob Burckhardt.

Christian mysticism has always been dominated by the authoritative style of Christianity. This is most evident in the writings of the greatest Catholic mystic, St. John of the Cross. It is astonishing to see how rigid spiritual systems can be put forth by someone who is said to be profoundly spiritual in his feelings. Protestant mystics are less afflicted by this tendency, but they still cannot escape relying on the dogma of Jesus Christ, the only Savior for mankind.

Dogmas are the death of development of one's own soul, which is all that a human being can ever expect to accomplish in 'the realm of spirit.' When this does not occur, the realm of Caesar takes over, as the case with most people today. The realm of Caesar is very powerful. Which is why I, Leon Landesman, have turned to the life of a solitary philosopher and have continued with it for many years. The damage done to my soul by the realm of Caesar has taken a long time to overcome.

> It is in man's nature, when he feels lost in the great, hectic, outside world, that he

should seek to find his own self in solitude. And the more deeply he has felt the inward division and destruction, the more absolute is the solitude he needs.

Jacob Burckhardt in *Die Zeit Constantins des Grossen*
(my translation)

~ 56 ~

The common feeling about mysticism is that it is seeking spiritual union with God—or however one wishes to name an all-embracing ground of spiritual reality. Holy, sacred, reverent, loving are predicates applied to the feelings connected with this union. My idea of mysticism is different. My mystical search is for *consciousness* of my own soul, for *formation* of my soul. I crave development of my inner spiritual substance. I accept the predicates but apply them to consciousness of my soul. Theologians might say I am seeking God without knowing it, but that would be their concept rather than my inner reality. I do not want concepts, I want only development and consciousness of the spiritual reality I call my soul. Whether it is coextensive with 'God' or not, I leave to the theologians whose business it is to generate concepts about God.

However, I think grave consequences ensue when an individual in the course of his mysticism thinks he has found God. It is only a short step then to thinking he knows the will of God. When people think they know the will of God, watch out! Soon they will expect you to follow his will—and if you don't, anything can happen. Today, Islamic fanatics have replaced with their own murderous brand the Christian violence of yesteryear; but even without murder, serious damage can be inflicted in many ways on the body or psyche of nonbelievers.

More relevant in today's world is the belief that mysticism is a form of superstition holding back one's intellect. If you don't take ideas of the soul or that of God seriously, there is no point engaging in the type of meditation that qualifies as mystical thinking. It serves no useful purpose. Your consciousness will be confined to objects in the material world (including persons as objects), and to feelings or concepts about them. Without spiritual awareness, the personality of a human being becomes two-dimensional in nature.

I think the main reason it is difficult to maintain a genuine interest in mystical thought is that survival is dependent on consciousness of the material world. This is true of all animals, including the human animal. If one looks carefully at the behavior of animals, even domestic ones, one can see how alert they are to the circumstances of their environment. The slightest change causes them to take notice, and how when they are going about their affairs, they still notice their physical environment. Human beings are the same, albeit in more subtle and comprehensive ways. There is constant pressure to pay attention to the material world surrounding them. Consequently, the fragile spiritual consciousness is difficult to maintain. Human beings are really not spiritual creatures; this development is of recent origin and questionable permanence.

I doubt that there is an appreciable difference between real philosophy and theology. One inevitably leads to the other. All the great theologians—Augustine, Aquinas, Spinoza, Hegel (God as Absolute Spirit), Kierkegaard, Berdyaev, Tillich, just to name a few—were equally philosophers. Even the French intellectuals who rejected the Judeo-Christian God—Voltaire, Rousseau, Diderot, and later, Sartre, and Camus—were theologians of a sort, 'negative theologians.' Militant atheists assert nothing can be known about God and if he exists he has nothing to do with human beings. This attitude reveals their metaphysical limitations. The main distinction between philosophers and religious theologians is that the latter depend upon a mystical *revealed* knowledge of God coming from outside themselves. Usually this revelation comes as confirmation of a traditional theology, but sometimes is unique in itself. In the case of Hindu Vedanta, there is absolutely no distinction between its philosophy and theology. The theology of Buddhism is entirely negative in nature, which is why Buddhism is said to have no God.

I don't argue with the revelations of others, but I can't put any trust in revelations that I have not experienced myself. There is no point saying to me, "believe first and then understanding will follow." This seems to me one of the most absurd ideas ever put forth by serious thinkers. From a psychological point of view, it is the height of naiveté. Of course, if one has religious faith, he will eventually construct a system of thought to fit his faith, especially if the faith is comforting to him. But that does not vouch for its truth. The most that can be said is that it might have the pragmatic value accorded to faith by William James. However, I don't crave pragmatic 'truth'; I want the real thing. The only 'Kingdom of God' that has been revealed to me is the soul within me (Luke 17:21). That's my theology.

~ 57 ~

English writers have a great advantage over their American counterparts. They have a way with their native language that Americans just do not. Whenever I read something that exhibits exceptional style and grace of expression, I think this must be an Englishman who has written it. Nine times out of ten, I am right. English writers in the past have been gentlemen and have written accordingly. None of the Hemingway style with its crude terseness would do for English writers. (I can't say, however, what writing is like at the present time in England.) I myself cannot begin to match writers like George Gissing or W. Somerset Maugham for elegance of expression.

Unfortunately, when it comes to philosophy, the English along with the Americans have chosen to emulate German philosophical esotericism. The English philosopher F. C. S. Schiller bemoaned this trend, saying philosophy used to be a subject that educated gentlemen could read with pleasure. Pleasure indeed! Reading contemporary philosophy for the uninitiated is an exercise in self-flagellation.

~ 58 ~

I enjoy reading great philosophers of antiquity whose writings have managed to survive up to the present time. Epicurus, Epictetus, Seneca, and Marcus Aurelius fall into this category. It gives me a feeling of continuity with humanity. The philosophers I have mentioned are human beings like myself and know how to project their humanness into their writings—or in the case of Epictetus, his transcribed lectures. The feelings and thoughts they describe are feelings and thoughts I have had. They help me think that I am not some sort of unfavorable mutation that has appeared on the earth by accident. They know about the soul and their souls are like my soul. Even though we are separated in time by some two thousand years and their racial origins—and DNA I presume—have no relationship to mine, we share a common bond; we are philosophers of the soul.

~ 59 ~

My feeling about scholars of classical philosophy has always troubled me. No doubt this is because I am dependent upon them. I need the assiduous scholarly studies that they publish on the life and work of the great and not so great figures in the history of philosophy. Most importantly, I need their translations from languages I either do not know or of which I have an imperfect knowledge. What would I know about Greek and Roman antiquity without the translations scholars have made from Greek and Latin? There would be only secondhand discussions from which I learn little. The same is true of the Russian writers who have so heavily influenced me. I can manage most modern European languages, yet it is always with a sense of pleasure when I pick up a reliable translation.

I think what disturbs me is when scholars pass judgments on the subjects of their studies or of their translations. Often I feel that they miss the essential substance of the writers they analyze or translate. It may be impossible to approach philosophy analytically as is required of scholars and still respond *existentially* to them. One could not analyze the Gospels in a scholarly manner and still respond spiritually to them. The same is true of all the important writings in philosophy and theology. A scholar is like a professional waiter bringing fine foods to the dining table; he may know their names, how they were prepared, the nature of their constituents, and what their flavors are supposed to be, but he cannot know the special experiences of dining delight.

~ 60 ~

The skies over the forest were entirely overcast during my morning walk today. Usually the weather here in the morning is sunny and breezy, quite bracing, causing Amigo and myself to walk with a brisk pace. But today, the air was still and the skies were sullen. Often a tropical storm far off the coast of Baja California causes this type of weather.

Thunderstorms and intense rain may follow. It is surprising to me how much my mood is affected by such overcast skies. My usually calm self is replaced by a gloomy feeling that will not go away. I imagine the worst about everything, especially my life and my behavior. What can I make of this? It must be that my personality is not nearly as independent and stable as I think if something as evanescent as the weather can affect it so deeply.

I have to be realistic about myself. Changeability seems to be a principal feature of my mind. It reflects the reality that I am just a chip carried along by the torrent of time in a vast, unpredictable universe. There is no point in taking myself too seriously. My life can end at any moment and that will be the end of things. Dissolution of my soul or union with the ultimate ground of reality—who can say which is true? It is all well and good for me to nourish the 'God' within me, but it is absurd to believe I can know the overarching scheme of the universe. The Stoic philosophers were right: follow your own nature, make your own choices, then *amor fati*—and let the devil take the hindmost! (the latter phrase my own addition). It is not for we poor specimens of humanity to decipher all the mysteries of the world in which we live.

~ 61 ~

The writings of the Genevan philosopher Henri-Frédéric Amiel (1821–1881) have always interested me. I think it is because he wrote a *Journal Intime* of more than 17,000 pages filling 170 bound notebooks on subjects close to my heart. Of course, my journal intime cannot begin to compare with his in size and scope. Lately, I have been reading him again to see what I can learn. I have to make do with abridged versions that I have obtained over the years. The best discussion of Amiel and his journal is by Bernard Bouvier in his abridged edition of 1923. (Unfortunately I only have a Spanish translation.) *L'Age d'Homme,* a Swiss publisher, has brought out the entire *Journal* in numerous volumes at a cost prohibitive for me.

There is no interest in Amiel today outside of a few academic specialists in French literature so that his writings are hard to come by. This is not surprising since his extreme introspective style does not suit contemporary tastes. He gets no mention in English language philosophy texts because he is viewed as a memoirist rather than philosopher. I only became aware of him because of my inveterate habit in my former life of browsing through used bookstores. This would be impossible for me today as used bookstores seem to be rapidly going out of existence.

In spite of the limited availability of Amiel's writings, certain things have emerged in my mind about him. Whatever his personal limitations—and there were many, as he himself recognized in the journal—he valued his own soul and devoted his literary energies on it right up to the end of his life (His meditations during the last few days of his life are remarkable.) His critics have accused him of inordinate egocentricity, failure to develop a coherent philosophy, and refusal to engage in life's activities. A detractor has labeled him *ce bavard impénitent*, this impenitent chatterbox. And so he sometimes seems to be. But Amiel in the totality of his writings revealed all the complexities that can exist within an intelligent and cultured person, something that is very rare in any literature. There are many coherent philosophers and *engagé* writers, but there is no portrait of a deeply thoughtful soul to compare with that of Amiel.

There is an Emersonian quality to Amiel that appeals to me. One could describe his conception of Deity as the *Over-Soul*. But Amiel is more attuned to his human frailties than was Emerson and describes a broader scope for the human condition. I need to concentrate more on what he has to say in his *Journal Intime*. Reading Amiel is more worthwhile for me than are most other litterateurs or philosophers.

~ 62 ~

Yesterday I had the first premonitions of my mortality. While walking, I suddenly felt dizzy and had to sit down on a log. When I tried to call Amigo to return to me, I couldn't pronounce his name. My speech had become slurred, and try as I might, I couldn't get out his name. Besides all that, my right hand felt funny when I wanted to pick up his leash that had fallen to the ground.

I knew what these things meant. They were signs of an impending apoplexy. Once when I needed a physical examination to work at the post office, a doctor told me my blood pressure was elevated. He said I might need medications and to see my own physician, which I didn't do since I didn't have my own physician. I have not been examined by another doctor since that time, over twenty-five years ago. My health has always been sterling. But now, with these ominous signs, I remembered that episode.

I made it back to the cabin without further difficulty. Now I had to decide what to do. I have a Medicare card that I have never used, but I knew it entitled me to medical care. I would have to go to Tucson and find a doctor. Probably he would find my blood pressure elevated, and then would start the round of X-rays, laboratory tests, medications, return visits, and who knows what else. My life would be drastically altered. I feared apoplexy, but I feared more the thought of becoming a prisoner of the medical establishment.

I took thought of myself: I have passed the three score and ten years that is the allotted time span for an individual. My life has been a full one with more than the usual quota of intense experiences. Now I was on a downhill course; my eyesight was fading, my hearing was not what it used to be, I could no longer walk up to the top of the forest ridges without becoming breathless. Other, more intimate, deficiencies need not be mentioned. Why should I go through all the trouble and expense to prolong a life that was entering its final stage? Besides the trouble to me, there would be the mind-boggling costs of medical care, which even if I did not bear myself, would be borne by others. In good conscience, could I pass on these expenses of questionable value to taxpayers? All these thoughts went through my mind as I mulled over what to do. Finally, I came to a decision; I would let nature take its course. If I were fated to die of apoplexy, so be it; I would not become a burden to myself and to the world. I had a bottle of sleeping pills I had acquired during my student days. These could be used to hasten my end, if I became incapacitated. I make sure to have them always handy at my bedside with a water bottle.

It has been two weeks and my symptoms have not recurred. I am not at all worried; if the circulation to my brain gives out, I am quite prepared for it. I have no regrets about staying away from the medical profession. In some ways, I am looking forward to the great final event of my life, because perhaps then I will learn the answers to the questions that have been perplexing me.

~ 63 ~

Seneca for our Age. The Greek philosophers of antiquity lived in a world strange to us, but the Roman society of the first century A.D. bears an uncanny resemblance to America of the twenty-first century. Thus, it is worthwhile to pay attention to an exceptionally intelligent representative of that era, Seneca (4 B.C.–65 A.D.), and to listen from the perspective of two thousand years later to what he had to say. Distance lends validity to the thoughts of a discerning individual. Seneca's life spanned that of Jesus of Nazareth and of Paul of Tarsus; thus, what he tells us sheds light on many of the issues facing the founders of Christianity. In fact, a correspondence between Seneca and Paul supposedly emerged in antiquity, which only recently has thought to be spurious.

Seneca by birth came from a distinguished Roman family living in Cordoba, Spain, which produced other distinguished individuals. His well-known father Seneca the Elder, after whom he was named, wrote important handbooks on rhetoric, something in which his son excelled. An elder brother, Gallio, is named in *Acts of the Apostles,* because St. Paul appeared before him as procurator of Achaea. Gallio is depicted as not unsympathetic to Paul. A nephew of Seneca, Lucan, has been regarded as one of the classic poets of Latin literature, close to Virgil and Horace in importance.

The life of Seneca makes the most lurid Hollywood epic seem tame by comparison. He quickly became a highly successful orator and lawyer, accumulating a large fortune in the process. At age 37, he held a quaestorship, the initial administrative step to a career in high office. However, he incurred the enmity of the lunatic Roman emperor Caligula, who, it is said, only held back from having him murdered because he was led to believe that the asthmatic Seneca would soon die a natural death. However, Seneca did not die; but a few years later, another emperor, Claudius, banished him to Corsica because he had also incurred the enmity of that emperor. All this was a consequence of the vicious court intrigues of the Roman Empire.

During his eight years of forced exile in Corsica, Seneca initiated his literary career. He wrote plays, essays, and dialogues. All of these writings are suffused with the

Stoic philosophy, which Seneca favored early in his life. His writings reached Rome and achieved considerable popularity, so much so that he became the object of envious criticism by many prominent Romans besides emperors. His most important writing, however, is the *Moral Epistles*, many of which are really essays and only minimally concerned with morality in the contemporary sense of the word. These were written in the last years of his life.

In 49 A.D., an aristocratic Roman matron named Agrippina had him recalled from banishment in order to serve as tutor to her son Nero. It seems that Seneca did not have much choice in the matter if he wanted to escape Corsica. Nero became emperor in 54 A.D., with Seneca continuing to serve as his advisor. It is not clear if Seneca had much choice in this matter either. In any case, it is said that Seneca was virtually 'prime minister' of the Roman Empire during Nero's adolescence. But in 59 A.D., Nero's malignant nature emerged; he had his mother and brother murdered, revealing that Seneca had lost his influence over Nero. Seneca went into retirement in 62 A.D., spending his time on his estates and writing the *Moral Epistles*, supposedly to a young friend Lucilius. In 65 A.D., Nero suspected him of participating in a conspiracy against the life of the emperor. He dispatched centurions to find him with instructions to demand his suicide or else, a not uncommon habit of Nero at that time. Seneca carried out his suicide by severing arteries in his arms followed by suffocation in a steam bath. His young wife Paulina insisted in joining him in death, but she survived. There is general agreement that Seneca died bravely at 69 years of age in the best Stoic tradition.

Seneca is classified as a Stoic philosopher and the thought of this school had a major impact on him, but he certainly created his own brand of Stoicism. He often quotes Epicurus, the leader of an archrival sect of Stoicism in the antique world. Seneca is partial to poetry; the hardly stoical Homer and Vergil are constantly quoted. Christians have been tempted to claim him as their own because of his metaphysical and moral inclinations; the spurious Seneca-Paul letters were used to support this idea. But mainly Seneca is original; his style of writing with its personal qualities is unique for his times. Not until Augustine, centuries later, will a 'philosopher' emerge with a similar existential approach.

The central focus for Seneca is the human soul. If one does not accept the existence of the soul, he will gain little from Seneca. For this philosopher, the most important task for a human being is development and preservation of his soul—not an easy task in the Roman Empire of his day. "The human soul is a great and noble thing, it permits of no limits except those shared by the Gods" (Ep. 102). He would have whole-heartedly subscribed to the maxim of Jesus, "For what is a man profited, if he shall gain the whole world and lose his own soul." Much in the *Letters* emphasize the futility of trying to gain the things the world has to offer and their destructive impact upon one's soul. "The soul, I affirm, knows that riches are stored up elsewhere than in men's heaped-up treasure-houses; that it is the soul and not the strongbox, which should be filled" (Ep. 92). He inveighs especially against the evils arising from slavery, gladiatorial games, and unrestrained luxury—features that characterized the materialist ethos of the Roman Empire.

The problem of death greatly occupied Seneca's mind. He does not understand how rational individuals who know that every life must be terminated by death can be so overwrought by its occurrence. He says one should rather be grateful for having had a life, regardless of its length, instead of bemoaning its end; when, in fact, it may be a new beginning for the soul. He is all for voluntary termination of life, if this seems appropriate. The following quote could serve as a moral guide for this issue today:

> I shall not abandon old age, if old age preserves me intact for myself, and intact as regards the better part of myself; but if old age begins to shatter my mind, and to pull its various faculties to pieces, if it leaves me

> not life but only the breath [shadow] of life, I shall rush out of a house that is crumbling and tottering. I shall not avoid illness by seeking death, so long as the illness is curable and does not impede my soul. I shall not lay violent hands on myself just because I am in pain; for death under such circumstances is defeat. But if I find out the pain must be always endured, I shall depart, not because of the pain, but because it will be a hindrance to me as regards all my reasons for living. He who dies just because he is in pain is a weakling, a coward; but he who lives merely to brave out his pain is a fool.
>
> (Ep. 58–trans. Richard Gummere)

Seneca has been subjected to severe criticisms, both in his day and ours. His literary peers did not see him as a Stoic philosopher; they saw him as a wealthy lawyer maneuvering for high office, as a sycophant to emperors, as advisor to one of the most vicious emperors ever to occupy that post. Some saw him as an unscrupulous hypocrite. Such judgments have been carried over to our time. A recent biography of him by an academic essentially echoes these opinions. (I wonder why someone who thought so poorly of Seneca would spend so much time writing his biography—academic advancement I suppose.) Moreover, his style of writing—so-called silver point—has been criticized as sententious and manneristic. His clipped Latin syntax, often using one word for the English three, renders the impression of a series of sententiae (personally, I admire insightful sententiae and I like Seneca's style).

Regarding sycophancy, it is hard to envision Seneca fawning too much on emperors when he was exiled by one of them and marked for death by two others—the last one carried out. Unlike other Stoic philosophers, Seneca moved in the highest circles of the empire because of his family background; he became involved with Nero only because he could not have escaped exile otherwise. I imagine it is hard for an academic in a snug little university office to empathize with someone like Seneca living amidst the ruthless brutality and corruption of the Roman Empire of that era. We should be interested in Seneca the philosopher, not Seneca the reluctant advisor to Nero, nor as the wealthy Roman man of affairs. Henry David Thoreau who was the soul of integrity had this to say about himself in a letter to a friend: "My actual life is a fact in view of which, I have no occasion to congratulate myself, but for my faith and aspiration I have respect. It is from these that I speak." We should listen to Seneca for his faith and aspirations, not the uncertain details of a life two thousand years ago.

As far as the accusation of hypocrisy is concerned, let him who is without sin cast the first stone. The founders of Christianity, Paul and Augustine, had much to be ashamed of in their early lives. Who better than Seneca knew about the excesses in his society and its need for spiritual rejuvenation? The sincerity of the *Moral Epistles* seems evident to me; others can make their own judgments. What is unquestioned is that Seneca met his fate in a manner worthy of the highest standard of a philosopher.

Seneca has much to offer our society. His commitment to a spiritual interior self, to combating the evil effects of opulence and unrestrained hedonism, to opposing the irrational fear of death, and to the need for a personal philosophy at all ages and in all eras is exactly what is needed today to counteract the spiritually destructive way of modern living. May he exert his influence more in the future than he has in the recent past. Here are some 'sententiae' of Seneca from the *Epistulae Morales* of the Loeb Classical Library of Heinemann-Harvard (English translations by Richard Gummere):

Ep. 20: Philosophy teaches us to act not to speak.
Facere docet philosophia, non dicere.

Ep. 7: It is necessary either to imitate or to loathe the world.
Necesse est aut imiterus aut oderis.

Ep. 6: I have begun to be a friend to myself.
Amicus esse mihi coepi.

Ep. 49: The language of truth is simple.
Veritatis simplex oratio est.

Ep. 74: Let us limit the supreme good to the soul.
Summum bonum in animo contineamus.

Ep. 74: Love reason!
Ama rationem!

Ep. 95: When the learned appear, good men are lacking.
Postquam docti proderunt, boni desunt.

Ep. 75: Our affair here is with the soul.
Hic animi negotium agitur.

Ep. 76: Therefore, that alone is good which will make the soul better.
Ergo unum id bonum est, quo melior animus efficietur.

Ep. 82: Leisure without literature is death, a tomb for a living man.
Otium sine litteris mors est et hominis vivi sepulta.

Ep. 88: I respect no study, and deem no study good, which results in money-making.
Nullum in bonis numero, quod ad aes exit.

Ep. 92: It is the soul, and not the strongbox, which should be filled.
Animum impleri debere, non arcam.

Ep. 124: You will come to your own when you shall understand that those whom the world calls fortunate are really the most unfortunate of all.
Tunc habemis tuum, cum intelleges infelicissimos esse felices.

~ 64 ~

As I grow older and gain experience of life, I have come to believe that there is one single critical issue that determines the character of an individual—and that is whether he is aware of the existence of his own soul. He may not consciously and explicitly formulate the awareness, but if it exists in the depths of his self, it will affect his entire life. If he lacks this awareness, consciously or subconsciously, he will be at the mercy of all the pressures of society inhibiting his personal development. Reverence for one's soul—that is the key for success in life. How does one gauge success? Seneca at the end of the last letter of the *Moral Epistles* gives a brief rule of thumb, "You will come into your own when you understand that those who are thought to be 'successful' are the most unsuccessful."

We don't think well enough of our interior selves—always looking for accomplishments, possessions, recognition, praise by others. These goals may be superficially appropriate at various times for our superficial selves, but not for our own *essential* selves, our souls. Here belongs the saying of Feuerbach from the *Essence of Christianity*, Chap. V. "That *alone is holy* to man which lies deepest within him, which is most peculiarly his own, the basis, the essence of his individuality" (italics mine). A person must *revere* his essential self; denying this reverence is catastrophic for the development of the individual. "Let he who has ears, hear."

I will review for myself my concepts of the development of the soul. First and foremost, the soul is a metaphysical entity and must be considered in that light—whatever the nature of its relationship to the physical brain. Initially, in a fetus, it is a potentiality, not an actuality, if I may borrow terminology from Thomas Aquinas. Unlike Catholic dogma, however, I think there is a fundamental difference between potentiality and actuality. The fetus has no soul. But once it breaks the umbilical bond with the mother, it becomes capable of using its senses to experience the world; it begins to form its soul. When an infant becomes mobile, the range of experience is greatly extended. It begins to learn about the distinction between itself and the outer world. All this has been studied in detail by developmental psychologists. Thus, the soul's formation is accelerated.

When a child begins to acquire language, the theater of its activity becomes infinitely enlarged. It learns about the connection of symbols to reality. Other people assume a greater significance than just a source of sensory stimuli. The nature of the world around it takes shape. Much later it may learn about the *meaning* of what he or she experiences. Concept and value formation occurs. The soul becomes more clearly defined. Without being conscious of it, the maturing individual grows his soul.

For better or for worse, family life provides the initial model for social development of a child. The habits, activities, interests, and values provide models on which a child develops his social persona. In time, friends and school provide additional models, but the initial formative influence of the family is very strong. Ultimately, the potentiality of a soul in a newborn infant becomes an actuality in the individual. But sometimes the potentiality remains undeveloped and the individual remains tied to his surroundings just as a fetus is to the uterus.

Free will is the essential correlate of spiritual development. It too requires a model for its development. One has great difficulty in achieving personal success without some kind of spiritual model upon which to create this success. Plato needed the model of Socrates upon which to build his philosophical persona; St. Paul needed his vision of Jesus to create Christianity; and St. Augustine needed the model of his mother to go forward in his religious development. This is why antique thinkers put so much emphasis on philosophical lineage. It is only a rare individual who can fully develop his soul without a model to grow upon. Consequently, the spiritual poverty of the current era.

Seneca, who had the model of his father upon which to develop his rhetorical skills, has provided an insight that is as pertinent to our times as it was to his:

> Our parents have instilled into us a respect for gold and silver; in our early years the craving has been implanted, settling deep within us and growing with our growth. Then too the whole nation, though at odds on every other subject, agrees upon this; this is what they regard, this what they dedicate to the gods when they wish to show their gratitude—as if it were the greatest of all man's possessions! And finally, public opinion has come to such a pass that poverty is a hissing and a reproach, despised by the rich and loathed by the poor.
>
> *Epistulae Morales,* #115 (Loeb Library, Harvard Univ. Press)

The models of our era are almost entirely material in nature. Thus, we are in the process of becoming robots entirely subjected to the causality principle of material existence. Only lip service is paid to the soul out of deference to habit and long dead traditions. Most people do not even grasp what the term *soul* signifies. Like the concept of God, to which it is related, the meaning of soul approaches the ineffable; various predicates can be applied to it but they do not define the soul. But without consciousness of its presence, its potentiality disappears. A person becomes what he thinks; materialists become alternately merchants and merchandise. "Things are in the saddle, and ride mankind," Emerson wrote. *Homo sapiens* reverts to *Homo faber*, a tool making and using creature, rather than a spiritually creative one. The only alternative to robotic existence is to develop and revere the God-like soul within one.

The person drawn to mystical thinking must realize there are some things for which language does not suffice. It has been long known that awareness thought to derive from God falls into that category. This is what is meant by the term *ineffable*. But it is also true that awareness having to do with the soul is similar in nature. Language does not suffice for its description or definition. This does not mean one has to be silent on the subject, as Ludwig Wittgenstein asserted at the end of his famed *Tractatus Logico-Philosophicus*. A person conscious of his soul ought to speak out to the best of his ability. Even if what is said does not meet with the approval of logical purists or dogmatic materialists, it does remind oneself that his soul exists. It gives his words an importance far beyond the unidimensional ruminations of logicians and materialists.

~ 65 ~

Some time ago when I was returning from my walk with Amigo, I saw an unfamiliar car parked in front of my doorway. It was not a Border Patrol vehicle. I felt some trepidation and sensed my heart rate speeding up, something I don't like to happen. Could it be a Cartel vehicle coming to settle scores with me because of Gustavo's departure? Such things have happened. Anyway, I mustered up my courage and approached the car. There were two men in it. "Are you looking for something?" I said with a firmness I really did not feel. The men got out of the car and I could immediately tell they were not Cartel representatives. One came up to me with a big smile and an outstretched hand. "How are you today, Mr. Landesman?" he said. I always ignore outstretched hands of people I don't know. "What do you want?" I responded brusquely.

Well, that triggered a long song and dance from him about that he was a journalist from the Tucson Herald newspaper, that the paper had heard that I was a philosopher leading an unusual life next to the National Forest, and that he hoped I would be willing to give him an interview since he knew that their readers would be fascinated by the story. The other man was his photographer to take photos of myself, my cabin, and even my dog. I might find the publicity helpful to my career. For the first time, I noticed the PRESS placard on the windshield of their car.

I took a deep breath and tried to be civil. "I have no career. I am sorry to disappoint you but I don't give interviews and I forbid any pictures of my property appearing in your newspaper. Now if you will excuse me, my dog is waiting for his morning meal." I turned on my heels, entered my house, and locked the door, something I rarely do. It took a while, but finally I heard their car drive away.

Although the episode did not last more than ten minutes, it disturbed my mental equilibrium for the rest of the morning. I could not concentrate on my writing. Years ago when a tour bus stopped at my cabin, discharging a horde of gabbling women, I was so disjointed that it took days for me to recover. I suppose I am too hypersensitive to intrusions into my personal space. It would be better if I were thicker skinned, but that is the way I am. That's why I live the way I do.

~ 66 ~

I am reading Seneca in my spare time—or I should say rereading him since I have spent much time with him in previous years. I find it quite enjoyable to read the Moral

Epistles, especially the Gummere translation in the Loeb Classical Library series. Probably the only other readers of these books are Latin scholars. But it appeals to me to read Seneca because of his devotion to his idea of the human soul and to philosophy in general (as it was in his times). The facing Latin gives me the opportunity to brush up on the language that served as the main vehicle of western culture for over a thousand years. My mother had arranged for me to study Latin with a private tutor when I was in high school, but I heedlessly let the language lapse in subsequent years. Now I am having the pleasure of renewing my association with an old friend.

Seneca brings his spiritual humanism to bear on the habits and customs of the Roman Empire of his day. He especially had an enlightened attitude toward slavery, which was prevalent throughout antiquity. He railed against cruel treatment of household slaves, feeling they should be treated with dignity, as if they were part of the household. Some of the descriptions he gives of sadistic treatment of slaves are horrifying. Seneca emphasizes the fact that slaves and masters are equally human beings and, in fact, their roles could be reversed if fate so ordained. He mentions prominent philosophers such as Plato and Diogenes who were slaves at one time.

Yet it never seemed to occur to Seneca to criticize the *institution* of slavery. He seems to accept it as a given in the world. I attribute this surprising shortcoming to his privileged position. It put blinders on him with respect to slavery as an institution. This is the problem with privileged positions in any era; it puts blinders on the individual. During the era of slavery in the United States, the privileged elite of the South did not see slavery for what it was. This country is still paying for that blindness. Today, privileged Americans do not see the militarism and economic imperialism of their country as it is exerted over many parts of the world. Our descendants will in turn pay dearly for this blindness.

~ 67 ~

I, Leon Landesman, have no discernable spiritual past. This reality has been dawning on me more and more recently. I was an adopted orphan, who had no knowledge of his biological parents. My adoptive parents, one a Jewish atheist and the other a secular freethinker, brought me to America to escape Soviet tyranny. They wanted nothing to do with the languages or way of life that would remind them of the Russia they had escaped. The Soviets in turn had wanted nothing to do with the life under the Czars that they had replaced—and that had been the only true source of Russian culture. The upshot of it was that I inherited no ancestral traditions: not Russian, not Jewish, not Christian, nothing. I began my spiritual life from square one. I was totally dependent on my societal milieu to develop myself. And that source ultimately failed me.

I have been trying to determine the significance of having no spiritual past. This is not uncommon in the 'Golden Land,' where millions of nineteenth and early twentieth century immigrants wanted little or nothing to do with the life they had left behind. The languages were not transmitted—a most significant abandonment since language is the main vehicle for transmitting culture. Assimilation into the frenzied American life was all that counted. In my case, the abyss separating the old from the new was enormous: no ancestors, no language, no culture. Spiritually, as well as biologically, I was an orphan.

Returning to the question posed above: what is the significance of having no spiritual ancestry? In some ways it has been an advantage for me; there have been no moribund traditions to rid myself of, no restrictions on my freedom to read, write, and think. There has been no theological baggage to prevent me from striking out on my own, psychologically and spiritually. I am my own man in every way, a fact that has given me a feeling of much pride. As I look around, I see superannuated religious traditions responsible for the failure of spiritual development so prevalent in my society. The Judeo-Christian God may be dead, but the influence of His dead hand lives on.

The negative features of ancestral tradition have been easy for me to recognize, but the positive elements have been much more elusive. However, after considerable meditation, I have come to the realization that a person like myself, growing up without any spiritual tradition, is ultimately at a disadvantage in self-development. Those who have experienced nothing *spiritual* in their past have a harder time experiencing it in their present. They have not developed the awareness of *holiness*, which is what a living spiritual tradition fosters in the young. If one has not learned to feel anything to be holy in the world outside of himself, he will have great difficulty feeling anything to be holy within himself. He will be less likely to feel reverence for his own soul. This is a serious defect in a person.

The prevalent scientism of contemporary American society feeds into and maintains this defect in individuals. Intelligent scientists know they are only dealing with a segment of reality; philosophers are supposed to have the whole in mind. Modern philosophy has grievously failed at this responsibility. This failure strengthens the lack of awareness of spiritual reality that exists everywhere today. Mindless fundamentalist religion cannot remedy the situation; it only makes it worse since there is no magical 'born again through Jesus,' there is only the slow process of developing one's interior spiritual self. Nicholas Berdyaev in his usual forceful manner has written, "Man has ceased to understand why he is living; he has not time to meditate on the meaning of life. Man's life is filled with means for living, which means have become ends in themselves" (*The Realm of Spirit and the Realm of Caesar*). This is the whole story of the materialist worldview. The latter half of my life represents my effort to counteract this doleful state of affairs in which I had found myself. I had no overarching desire to save humanity; I wanted only to save myself.

~ 68 ~

My philosopher friend and neighbor Richard Schain came by my cabin the other day. Usually he is on his morning walk and just goes by it, waving to me if I am outside. But this time he came to my door, wanting to talk to me. I invited him in.

"I have a proposal to make to you, Leon," he began. I thought that he was going to invite me to one of his parties again, which I already had decided to refuse. But after a few pleasantries, what he had to say startled me.

He began, "My wife and I are planning a trip to Europe for three months. We need a live-in person to look after the house and our dogs. I thought you would be the perfect person. You could use our kitchen and our laundry facilities, sleep in the guest room, watch our television and bring Amigo. My library would be at your disposal. I will provide you with a stipend for unexpected expenses, although, of course, that wouldn't be the main incentive for you. It could be a welcome break from your Spartan existence here. What do you think? Would you be interested?

This offer really took me by surprise. I didn't know what to think. Finally, I stammered out a response.

"That's very nice of you to trust me with your home, Richard. I just don't know. Can I think about it for a while?"

"Of course," he said. "But let me know soon, because if you don't want to do it, we'll have to find someone else. But I hope you do agree. I don't know of anyone in whom I would have more confidence to take care of my home and my two boys." He always referred to his dogs as his 'boys.' He whistled them up and went on his way.

The rest of the day I spent mulling over Richard's proposal. I must confess that at first, I was tempted to agree. I knew his house; it was more luxurious then anywhere I had ever lived. I would be able to browse in his large library, most of which were philosophy books. Also I was flattered that he thought so highly of me that he was willing to entrust his home and animals to my care. I didn't think he knew me that well. Perhaps I could use a break from my 'Spartan existence,' as he had put it. I had never thought of myself before as leading a Spartan existence.

Then my 'demon' began to emerge from its hiding place in my soul. Why should I want to return to a bourgeois existence, even temporarily, when such an existence drove me to the forest years ago? Could I be comfortable in such extravagant surroundings? Did I want to be enveloped by all that luxury and technology—surroundings that I felt had corrupted me in my former life. Even on a practical level, did I want to be responsible for all the gadgetry of his lavish home? The fact was that other than our interests in philosophy, our lives were worlds apart; there was no point of contact between them. If I physically entered Richard's world, who knows what would be the end of it? The discipline I have developed for my solitary existence might not return when I had to reenter it. I was older now and not as physically or mentally strong as when I first moved into my cabin. The more I mulled it over, the more I thought it to be a bad idea for me, a dangerous toying with my life. At the end, I resolved to refuse Richard's offer.

The simple life that Thoreau had recommended—and others like Seneca before him—is not so simple to achieve for someone who is a product of American life.

Thoreau did not hold out at Walden; Seneca with his slaves and villas never really knew the simple life. I feel that I am a pioneer in the art of developing one's soul in a spiritually deprived society. Like the former pioneers in this part of the world, there are very few who could endure the adversity. But I have endured and will continue to do so. My life reflects my thoughts and my thoughts reflect my way of life. Whatever others might think about my life, there is a meaning to it of which I am proud. Entering into Richard's bourgeois-oriented existence would endanger that meaning—something I am not willing to do.

~ 69 ~

I have been living an isolated life for quite a few years now. Usually I do not become intimate with others, but every so often someone will say something like the following to me: "Is your life not lonely, do you not miss the stimulation of human company, would you not like to have friends, if even only one companion in your life?" I try to answer as honestly as I can. My soul was starved when I was living my former life with friends, stimulation, and all the rest of social existence. I found it most unprofitable to have much to do with the human company that had been available to me. My past experiences have left me, as Thoreau says somewhere in his correspondence with H.G.O. Blake, with an insatiable appetite for solitude. I am stimulated by my own thoughts, which to paraphrase Thoreau again, are the only things of real significance in my life. All the rest is just the blowing of the wind.

Instead of friends, I have my library. The one worthwhile thing that has resulted from my past academic life was the acquisition of my library. It is not an ornament of my home as are so many libraries today; it is an essential component of my life. I have five hundred or so volumes, but there are only about twenty-five that are really important to me. Where would I find twenty-five friends in society; where would I find five? two? one? Periodically, I renew my acquaintanceship with one of them with great pleasure and profit. Just recently, I opened again my profusely underlined copy of *The Correspondence of Henry David Thoreau* (ed. Walter Harding and Carl Bode), which is why his thoughts are fresh in my mind. In my opinion, his exchanges with his friend H.G.O. Blake are the best sources of Thoreau's thoughts. No friend I could have had would have equaled the impact that Thoreau's thoughts have had upon me.

Some time ago, I had the disturbing experience of reading in *Lives of the Eminent Philosophers* by Diogenes Laertius—one of my twenty-five volumes—the following discussion: D.L. is relating an anecdote about Diogenes of

Sinope, the main figure of the Cynic movement in philosophy (no relation to D. L.). Hegesias, a philosopher contemporary with D.S., has asked Diogenes to lend him one of his writings (D. S. wrote books, but none have survived). Diogenes answered: "You are a fool Hegesias; you prefer real figs to the painted ones on strings, and yet you pass over my real life to study a string of writings." The genuine nature of some of D. L.'s anecdotes has been doubted by scholars, but this idea must have been prevalent in the philosophical circles of the times.

I have to admit this anecdote bothered me for some time. Was I avoiding "real life" by shutting myself up with books? Was I, like Hegesias, a fool for doing so? Gradually, however, the situation unfolded in my mind. If I would have had available to me the society of the ancient Greek philosophers, with its bold openness, I think I might have chosen that over forest solitude. But instead, all I had was a desiccated academia, more concerned with tenure and prestige than with development of their souls. They were no longer even aware of their souls; if they used the word, it was only in a joking or metaphorical manner. Greek philosophy was a means of demonstrating scholarly proficiency, not for personal development. Beyond academic philosophy, there was the social world of business, professions, politics—none of which had any appeal for me. My own thoughts, my library, and the forest were my refuge, and when I read in Thoreau's letters to Blake, "I have lately gotten back to that glorious society called Solitude," I felt confirmed in the way of life I had chosen.

Now, I don't mean to recommend my life for everyone. It is not for the youth or *hoi polloi* that populate societies everywhere. It is for a chosen few, the lucky ones, the ones who have learned how to build, fill, and utilize a "storehouse of their souls."

~ 70 ~

I am still 'learning' about my own life and my relationship to God and the world. There is so much to uncover. Atavistically, I follow the old Rabbinical maxim *"Men hot zu lernen"*—one must learn.

~ 71 ~

I much prefer Emerson's journal entries to his essays—the latter are more *literary and theoretical*, the former more *personal and incisive*. I especially am taken with the entries written during his Harvard student days when he was but 20 and 21 years of age. Their precocity is amazing. Once he entered the Divinity profession, he became more mentally conformist, less free in his expressions. Nevertheless, all Emerson's journals are worth reading.

[The following essay on the significance of philosophy seems to have been written during Landesman's tenure as a college professor. Apparently he was not successful at publishing it. It terminates his writings and I leave it to readers to judge its merit. – Ed.]

Richard Schain

TOWARD A PHILOSOPHICAL FAITH

"FAITH IS NOTHING ELSE than belief in the absolute reality of subjectivity." So stated Ludwig Feuerbach in his nineteenth century book *The Essence of Christianity* whose epochal concepts have yet to be incorporated into western culture. The title is somewhat misleading; the title Feuerbach originally proposed was "Critique of Pure Irrationality, the Correspondence of Religion with the Essence of Mankind," a ponderous title but one that is descriptive of its contents. Marketing problems, however, led Feuerbach's publisher to utilize the title under which it appeared, apparently with Feuerbach's consent. The book is now generally to be found in the religious section of bookstores.

It is noteworthy that about the time Feuerbach's book appeared, two other writers were producing their own epochal books with very different styles and interpretations but essentially endorsing the theme that subjectivity is what counts. These were Henry David Thoreau (*Walden*) and Søren Kierkegaard (*Concluding Unscientific Postscript*) whose lives and works were based on this belief. None of these writers knew of the existence of the others yet certain ideas in their work were astonishingly similar. Something in the *Zeitgeist* of the mid-nineteenth century was generating the intuition that "truth is in subjectivity."

In the contemporary era, there is little evidence that such an intuition has survived. The world is still bedeviled with the age-old habits of projecting the feelings of the inner self into outer objects of worship, if not a demanding Jehovah, then a stylish home or a state of the art automobile. Fanatical Islam is on the rise, threatening to displace the traditional Christianity of western societies. Individuals are still not capable of justifying their spirituality within themselves; there needs to be an external power or tradition legitimizing its existence. European philosophy as a guide to a higher life has been a failure and is now confined to university existence with philosophers playing roles of historians, teachers, or cognitive 'scientists'—in spite of the tirades of Schopenhauer and Nietzsche. Those philosophy professors who wish to express themselves on the human condition are now more inclined to demonstrate against racism or attack 'savage' capitalism than to speak to the issue of interior consciousness.

The individual who wishes to develop his soul, however, needs something more than political activism. He needs a way of life with values founded on his own subjectivity. The ancient Greeks did not feel it necessary to add that the *gnōthi seauton* would not occur without the *experiences* that teach the individual about himself. No one develops a fruitful subjectivity locked in a closet; the Puritans carrying the mission of the Reformation into a hostile wilderness had plenty of experiences through which their souls could grow. By the time of Emerson and Thoreau, however, it was becoming evident that American civilization did not value inner growth.

One might maintain that the art of human life lies in fostering the types of experiences that lead to interior development. Only the individual himself can intuit what kind of experience will be meaningful to him; what will lead to deepening of the soul in one individual may be tedious drudgery for another. Fulfillment for Thoreau came from solitary roaming in the woods of Concord; for Feuerbach, it was an intimate relationship with a young woman of exceptional spiritual qualities. Kierkegaard's formative experience in life was being son to a remarkable father; however one views this relationship, it left its imprint on Kierkegaard's soul. One might add the self-evident fact that fulfilling human experiences must involve one's physical being since the human condition does not permit any other means of experiencing the world.

Faith is more than a cognitive act of 'believing,' it is a commitment of the self to a set of *values* about one's own existence. Faith in the importance of the material world or faith in an almighty God or faith in creating one's own soul all produce different attitudes toward existence that affect every aspect of one's being. Humans cannot really live without any faith at all, although they can live without metaphysical belief systems. The gravest predicament in life, one that can lead to self-destruction, is to be left stranded without faith in anything. Faith is integral, it cannot be split into parts; the development of belief in one god instead of many gods was universally recognized as a higher type of religious belief. There is no logical reason why there should be only one god; there are many planetary bodies, why not many Gods? But something in the human psyche led to monotheism as minds matured. Perhaps this is because the source of religious sensibility is the integral human soul.

Dedication to one's own soul is as religiously significant as faith in any traditional god or god symbol. It is valuing and supporting its integrity that is the essential attribute of faith in the soul. Nietzsche wrote that the distinguished soul has 'reverence' for itself. Reverence does not permit soiling of the revered entity with misplaced beliefs or attitudes. *Homo sapiens* possess an *intellectual conscience* to avoid dishonoring one's soul. Belief in an almighty power who requires certain beliefs and behaviors of human beings dishonors the soul. No revelation has revealed to me whether or in what form God exists, but I do know that I exist and possess an interior spiritual reality called the soul. My faith is dedicated to this reality. I have no confidence in a metaphysics located outside of myself. Nor can I exactly define the nature of this metaphysical (synonym: spiritual) interior self that variably manifests itself as emotionality, desire, will, or most importantly, intelligent consciousness; but I know that it is there within me.

The manifestations of the soul are not static but change kaleidoscopically in their content and orientation. They may be affected by a moral sense in which case it is called moral conscience but this is not invariable. It is not important to produce a Gray's Anatomy of consciousness as the savants of phenomenology have tried to do. Consciousness in all its various dimensions ought not be an object of scholarly investigation; it is rather something to aspire toward with all one's energies. If purity of heart is to will one thing as Kierkegaard said, then the will toward a consciousness of reality is the philosopher's claim to philosophical purity.

If the development of a spiritual consciousness is the proper goal for individuals, then the prospects do not appear bright for *Homo sapiens*. Individuals seem more inclined to develop themselves as conquerors of nature than as devotees of their souls. It is hard to avoid the feeling that spiritual consciousness is disappearing.

Christianity, the major religious force in the world to date, has not provided a consciousness of spirituality that conforms to the requirement of reality. Christian faith, Christian hope, and Christian love are spiritual states but they are anchored to a cosmology that violates one's intellectual conscience. God is dead as a real force in the world for an increasing number of individuals. However, the materialist worldview, which is devoid of spirituality, is eminently believable. Nature is a tangible reality affecting the human state in many ways and science has learned how to successfully deal with nature. The more scientific technologies enter into the daily framework of human life, the more individuals become fixed to a materialist worldview. For those with a spiritual bent of mind, the human condition is unpromising. Robinson Jeffers felt that the human race was a failed experiment of nature; he concluded that a new start with a new model was needed.

But the single individual *qua* individual has nothing to do with the human race or any other abstraction referring to multitudes, whether the numbers are in the dozens or the billions. Even the family is an abstract concept without in-depth reality as far as the single individual is concerned. The unprecedented murderous violence of the German Third Reich could not be assimilated by shocked observers when presented as so many millions of people tortured, gassed, or shot. Viewing pictures was more significant and visiting concentration camps even more so. But most significant of all was the experience of a personal incarceration in the camps, which was an experience that changed the consciousness of the survivors forever. It is well known that experiences that do not destroy individuals, strengthen them.

If the proper study of mankind is man as Alexander Pope has written, the proper study of the individual is the self. Man the historian studies the course of mankind, man the individual studies himself—or other selves that teach him about himself. *Gnōthi seauton* (know yourself) is still the first and most important commandment of spiritual existence. The shifting currents of humanity on this planet are like the galaxies in the universe, they may be of interest from an abstract point of view but of no real significance for the individual. All the races, religions, and nations of man have no more meaning to me than do the extinct dinosaurs or the unborn races yet to emerge. This attitude called 'nominalism' by medieval scholastics is founded on the reality of individual existence, which is the main criterion by which individuals should regulate their lives.

The scriptural injunctions that Jesus identified as most important for right living were first to love God with all one's strength and second to love one's neighbor as one's self. But Jesus went beyond the scriptures; he asserted that the kingdom of heaven was *within* the individual. We must assume that Jesus did not regard his assertion as morally defective egocentricity; we think that he was announcing a new dimension in human spiritual history. Human activities based on external affairs are not part of this dimension; they are part of the world of externality that dominates other life forms. To be born again is to become spiritual, to turn inward. Society, family, occupation—all these have to do with the exterior self no matter how important they may seem. But when one turns within, a new world is found without limits; it is only necessary to have the willingness and the determination to explore it.

Philosophical faith is faith in the individual soul as the most important aspect of human existence. Subjectivity is not merely the antithesis of objectivity; it is consciousness of the internal dimension that is the special terrain of humanness. It is impossible to look within and without simultaneously with the same degree of intensity. When totally concentrating on the terrestrial object world, the interior dimension contracts and ultimately disappears. The person whose energies are habitually turned toward objectivity does not feel this dimension and regards it as illusory. If one's gaze is continually fixed on the outer world, he is confined to that world. The interior "kingdom" is perceptible only to those with the will and ability to fix a steady gaze upon it. It is not necessary to completely discount the significance of the external world, but that world is not the subject of this essay.

This discussion may seem to resemble a religious tract more than a philosophical statement. But there is no claim for a higher sanction for these thoughts; they represent a personal intuition of the writer on the nature of human existence. No God or Holy Spirit or evil power (hopefully not) is at work. The writing is the outcome of the expressive energies of the writer that wish to see the light of day. The fact that they have some kinship with Christian consciousness is evidence that there is a common reality, a shared *Logos*, which all spiritually oriented individuals carry. However, the writer feels no obligation to carry the excess baggage of Christianity, whether it be a brief Apostle's Creed or all the pronouncements of the Roman Catholic Church, *ex cathedra* and *urbi et orbi*, during two millennia of Christian history. Nor is he inclined to accept the bibliolatry of the Protestant sects since, to him, the thoughts of Jesus are a philosophical treasure from a human being like himself to be used according to his own lights. He is no more disposed to worship them than to worship any other treasure.

The essential element of philosophical faith is to rely upon the intuitions of the interior self; this makes it the most difficult of all faiths. However, a faith that is dependent upon societal traditions is not real faith. Faith has been defined by an early Christian writer as "being sure of what we hope and expect, of being certain of what we do not see" (Hebrews 11:1). This celebrated definition is surely another example of Scriptural naivety. Its virtue lies in its metaphysical acknowledgement, but the unknown writer then goes on to mention a long list of examples of faith that would be vetoed by the intellectual conscience of intelligent individuals today. Moreover, the presence of religious symbols, music or monuments, the emotional rewards of religious fellowship and, most especially, the derivation of concrete benefits from religious protestations do not strengthen faith, they corrupt it. One cannot speak of faith in an enterprise from which one obtains visible benefits. We live in an absurd world in which individuals say they have faith in activities that richly reward them materially. Levels of existence cannot be mixed any more than metaphors; it is improper to talk of faith when faith is providing material or social rewards to the individual.

The pioneer Puritans deceived themselves when they thought communal faith could be supported by visibly exposing the faithless in wooden stocks. Faith that cannot be maintained except through tangible rewards or punishments is not faith; it is adaptation to the environment. One must adapt to his environment but there is no point in calling such adaptation by other names. Kierkegaard recognized the absence of genuine faith in contemporary Christendom; it is difficult to understand why he persisted in trying to resuscitate a faith that was—and is—dependent on dogmas that are as defunct as any of the antique philosophical schools of Athens. When there is no viable basis to faith, faith *kata syneidēsin*—according to a higher consciousness—becomes defunct itself.

Philosophical faith is a consciousness and valuation of one's own soul. Consciousness of soul inevitably leads to concern for its wellbeing. There is very little in contemporary society to support wellbeing of the soul; one must create the conditions that maintain it, Don Quixote-like, driven by a personal intuition rather than by conformity to societal mores. Miguel de Unamuno said of Don Quixote that he taught the world how the individual spirit rises above ridicule and rejection. The image of the undaunted knight is one toward which an individual with a soul can aspire; it is only through renunciation of approval by society and distaste for its rewards that he is enabled to come to philosophical faith and thereby form his own soul.

END OF LANDESMAN'S LEGACY

Selected Writings by Richard Schain

Philosophical Artwork II (2017)
Landesman's Journal: Meditations of a Forest Philosopher (2016)
Toward an Existential Philosophy of the Soul (2014)
Souls Exist, 2nd Ed. (2013)
Interior Lights in a Dark Universe (2012)
Radical Metaphysics (2003)
The Legend of Nietzsche's Syphilis (2001)
Reverence for the Soul (2001)
Affirmations of Reality (1982)

RICHARD SCHAIN is an independent philosopher who divides his time between Alamos, Sonora, Mexico and Sonoita, Arizona, USA. He obtained A.B. (philosophy) and M.D. degrees from New York University. In a former life, Schain trained in neurology at the Yale Medical Center, later serving as professor of neurology and psychiatry at the University of California, Los Angeles. In the 1980s, he embarked on the life of a philosopher outside of academia. Schain lives with his wife Melanie Dreisbach who plays a significant role in all of his writings.

www.ingramcontent.com/pod-product-compliance
Lightning Source LLC
LaVergne TN
LVHW051118080426
835510LV00018B/2115